Victorian Townscape

Michael Millward and Brian Coe

VICTORIAN TOWNSCAPE

The Work of Samuel Smith

Ward Lock Limited, London

Contents

© WARD LOCK LIMITED, 1974

ISBN 0 7063 1855 2

First published in Great Britain 1974
by Ward Lock Limited, 116 Baker Street,
London W1M 2BB

All Rights Reserved.
No part of this publication may be
reproduced, stored in a retrieval system,
or transmitted, in any form or
by any means, electronic, mechanical,
photocopying, recording or otherwise,
without prior permission of
the Copyright owners.

Designed by Trevor Vincent.

Printed in Great Britain by
The Scolar Press Ltd, Ilkley, Yorks.
Bound by Webb Son & Co Ltd,
Ferndale, Glamorgan

Opposite
'Scene in Marshland during the Inundation of 1862'.
Illustration from Miller and Skertchly's
'Fenland Past and Present', 1878,
from a photograph by Samuel Smith (See p.8).

Plates 12 and 13 are from negatives in
the possession of Mrs Cartwright of Letchworth.
All other illustrations in the book are from negatives,
prints and documents in the Kodak Museum, Harrow,
and the Wisbech and Fenland Museum, Wisbech.

The end papers show a detail from
F. J. Utting's map of Wisbech, 1850,
photographed by Samuel Smith.

Preface

Towards the end of 1971 the Kodak Museum acquired a large number of paper negatives and prints by a then unidentified photographer. Since many were taken in and around Wisbech, in Cambridgeshire, the local museum—the Wisbech and Fenland Museum—was approached. They were able to identify the photographer as Samuel Smith, since they also possessed a collection of his negatives and prints. When all this material was brought together, it was evident that Smith, unknown until then outside his home town, was an early photographer of some significance. The two museums combined resources to present an exhibition of Smith's work, first in Wisbech in March 1973, then in London in May of that year. Subsequently, the exhibition was shown in the United States. This book presents a selection of the work of Smith, reproduced in facsimile, and it is hoped that it will help to give this talented Victorian photographer the recognition he deserves.

The majority of Smith's surviving photographs are held in the two collections. The Wisbech and Fenland Museum possesses 190 negatives, an album of 100 prints and a number of loose prints. The Kodak Museum has 125 negatives and some 70 mounted prints. There is a single Smith negative in the Royal Photographic Society's collection, and about twenty others are known to be in private hands. Peckover House, Wisbech, owned by the National Trust, has albums which include some of Smith's work, and there are other, privately owned, prints in the Wisbech area.

Most of Smith's pictures are of scenes in and around Wisbech, or within a few miles radius of the town. Occasionally, he made photograqhic excursions farther afield, to Ely, Hunstanton and Yarmouth, for example. At some time, possibly in 1860, he visited Yorkshire, perhaps on a visit to his married daughter who lived in the north. A number of the mounted prints in the Kodak Museum collection are of ruined abbeys, landscapes and other scenes in the West Riding. There are also a few prints of scenes in and near Conway, in north Wales, but these may not have been taken by Smith.

Almost all the plates in this book have been reproduced from prints made from the original negatives. A few have been made from copies of original prints.

Samuel Smith photographed with one of the microscopes
of his own construction, probably at the time of the
Wisbech Industrial and Fine Art Exhibition in
May 1866, at which he won an award for the microscopes
he exhibited.

Biography

After his death on 18 July 1892, the local paper recorded the following obituary:

On Monday night last there passed away to his rest a venerable and much esteemed neighbour, whose features were at one time very familiar in the streets of Wisbech, until advancing years compelled him to remain at home. Mr. Samuel Smith of Leverington Terrace, was familiarly known to his many friends as Mr. 'Philosopher' Smith, a complimentary allusion to his varied knowledge and love of investigation of various branches of science. He was an ardent collector and as a numismatist possessed an extensive knowledge of coins and tokens, his collection being a very valuable and interesting one. On this subject he was a contributor to Messrs. Miller and Skertchly's book *The Fenland*, and also to other works of a similar character. Nor was his knowledge confined to one or two branches, but his collection of specimens comprised valuable gems, a great variety of shells, and entomological specimens which he and Mrs. Smith had from time to time collected and examined under the lenses of a powerful microscope of his own construction. For many years, before age crept upon him, he was always ready at an art exhibition, conversazione or evening entertainment to take his microscopes and entertain many a visitor with the explanation of some pet object which he himself had mounted and prepared for the purpose. As a mechanic he was also very skillful, and an adept in the use of the lathe, with which he manufactured many useful additions for his cabinets and for the Wisbech Museum, of which he was always a kind and valued patron. In addition to his numismatic knowledge, he was also consulted upon geological and mineralogical specimens, and for many years, in company with the president, Mr. Algernon Peckover, attended weekly for the purposes of arranging the various objects, labelling them and adding to their own information respecting the contents of the cases. This friendly intimacy extended over a period of 30 years, and the curator, Mr. G. Oliver, informs us that so devoted was Mr. Smith to this congenial occupation, that he frequently took his lunch with him that he might be able to give more time to it. To Mr. Smith, the Museum is indebted for many of the coin trays made by himself with the aid of his lathe and other carpentry tools. He was an amateur photographer years before it was thought of as a fashionable pastime, and there are in existence today many old and interesting views of the river and old Wisbech which indicate the changes which time has made in the buildings and surroundings of our town and neighbourhood. One of the engravings in *Fenland* representing the famous Marshland Inundation of 1862 when the Middle Level Sluice gave way, is taken from a photograph by Mr. Smith. Although never taking an active part in public matters, he will be greatly missed by many who found in him a fund of information and scientific research. His good-humoured stories and conversation were always attractive to friends, who

never spent a pleasanter hour than when admiring his 'curios' and exploring the mysteries of his 'den'. Of a life distinguished by such versatile accomplishments as our late neighbour possessed, it is perhaps difficult to speak in the space of a brief notice, but many will recall reminiscences of his kindliness and readiness to give information and help, which will not be easily forgotten. Mr. Smith was twice married and his widow, who was a daughter of the late Mr. Thomas Dawbarn, J.P. survives him, as well as two daughters, one living in Wisbech—Mrs. Robert Bennett—and the other—Mrs. J. P. Halford—residing at Manchester. The funeral will take place on Friday next at the Leverington Road Cemetery.
(20 July 1892)

Gardiner's *History of Wisbech*, written a few years later, adds the following:—

The Rev. W. E. Winks, in his work entitled 'A Pastoral Medley' thus writes of the late Mr. Smith as 'My Philosopher Friend': 'A man of ample means and leisure, he had spent his time and gifts in out-door and in-door study, in collecting specimens, in the manufacture of scientific instruments. What was he? An astronomer? Yes, the best amateur astronomer I ever knew. When asked to show a particular nebula, cluster or double star, he would turn his four inch chromatic telescope upon it in a moment. A geologist? A mineralogist? A palaeontologist? Yes, he had worked in the field and the laboratory, and made his own wonderful collection, every specimen of which he could name at sight. A conchologist? To be sure. Look at these drawers of beautiful shells, and is not his collection of land and freshwater shells of the Fenland in the Wisbech Museum to this day? Ask him to show you his Hemiptera, Lepidoptera, &c., but not unless you are prepared to go through with them all. See how his eyes sparkle if you bring him a rare Greek, Roman, Byzantine, Ancient British, Saxon, Danish or English coin to look at and name for you. What are these tiny cabinets with their neat little drawers? Microscopic specimens—mineral, botanic, organic—prepared and mounted by himself, and shown in the fine microscope made with his own hands. Look at this little glass cistern full of ditch-water and its lenses at the end. Hear him discourse on the Rotifera, Amoeba, Cheironymous Lava; 'Dead as ditch-water!' I fancy I hear him say, 'Why it's one of the liveliest things I know, is a glass of ditch-water.'

Samuel Smith was a farmer's son, born in Tydd St Giles, the northernmost village in the Isle of Ely, about five miles from Wisbech. He does not appear in the register of baptisms in the parish church, which may mean that his father was a Dissenter. By 1830 he was in business as a timber merchant at March, Cambridgeshire, in partnership with John Smith, possibly his brother. He lived in Whittle End, March,

with his first wife, Myra, and two daughters. He is also listed in a directory of 1830 as a mechanist, a trade he put to good use in his later scientific pursuits.

The Smiths must have been successful, or perhaps inherited money, for by about 1847 Samuel had retired, well under fifty years old, to live at Malvern House, Leverington, a village about two miles from Wisbech and three from Tydd St Giles. John appears later as a timber merchant and keeper of the March Gas Works, although it is difficult to be sure with such a common name that he is the same one.

Samuel's wife died in November 1855 and he married again on 4 September 1860 to Frances Dawbarn at Hunstanton Parish Church.

Although he included many local public figures among his friends, he did not himself seek public office, and appears to have restricted himself to such activities as sitting on the committees of the Scientific Institution and the Museum at Wisbech, and membership of the Palaeontographical Society in London. He was a director of the Wisbech Gas Light & Coke Company, possibly on account of his expert knowledge.

His earliest dated photograph was taken on 12 October 1852, but he exhibited no photographs at the Public Hall Exhibition in 1853, of which he was one of the curators, and both he and Thomas Craddock were committee members. Smith showed 'an extensive collection of conchological specimens and minerals' and 'several curious philosophical instruments', while Craddock showed 'some choice calotypes' and 'richly illuminated missals'.

The portion of the room occupied by Mr. Smith's microscopes was a point of great attraction. Several most beautiful instruments of high magnifying power were brought into requisition the value of one of them being £100, and an almost illimitable variety of objects were presented from Mr. Smith's stores to the admiring gaze of the numerous visitors.
(*April 1853*)

By the following year he was more confident. When an exhibition was held of photographs from the Society of Arts of international architecture and scenery, also shown were

Some very beautiful examples of this locality, taken by Mr. T. Craddock and Mr. S. Smith, which were very much admired.
(*June 1854*)

In 1855, the following advertisement appeared:

VIEWS OF WISBECH: CALOTYPE VIEWS of the Old Bridge, the North and South Brinks, and various parts of the Town and neighbourhood, price 2/– each, may be had at the ADVERTISER office.
(*20 July 1855*)

These were quite possibly photographs by Smith or Craddock, and may indicate a direct business connection with the *Advertiser*.

That he was a well known and popular person is evident from what has already been said. After his death, the Museum Committee recorded the following tribute:

The Committee have to record with deep regret the death of their venerable colleague Mr. Samuel Smith in the 91st year of his age. Mr. Smith had been connected with this institution for nearly 44 years, and was indefatigable in his endeavours to benefit the Museum and promote its usefulness. He was always a welcome addition to their meetings, and his geniality and kindness endeared him to all. His place will in future be vacant, as it is impossible to find another so well versed in local antiquities, numismatics, the fauna and flora of the Fens and many kindred subjects in which a long life of careful patient observation had made him no mean authority.

Introduction

During the nineteenth century, as the industrial revolution drastically altered the traditional occupations and distribution of the population, profound changes began to occur in the urban environment of a sort which had not previously been experienced, but which became all too familiar in later years.

Documentation of change, taken for granted today, was rare in the middle of the last century. Although an ideal medium for recording change existed in photography, its potential was not widely realized at the time. Any substantial collection of Victorian photographs must have some relevance to the history of the locality in which they were taken. Change will have taken place since, and the photographs, if only by accident, will include things which no longer exist.

Samuel Smith made a record of Wisbech between 1852 and 1864 which we believe to be unique. While some of his work can be categorized, like so many early photographs, simply as technically excellent, well composed views, this does not adequately describe the photographs of the changing face of the town, in which he returned to a particular spot and set up his camera in an identical position to produce 'before and after' views. It is true he seems to have ignored certain aspects which are essential for a complete picture of the town, especially the canal and the railways, but despite these omissions, he was able to make a remarkably full record of Wisbech and the changes which took place in the 1850's. The relatively small size of the town enabled him to do this to an extent which would have been almost impossible in a large town or city.

Smith knew John Gardiner, proprietor and editor of the *Wisbech Advertiser*, and Thomas Craddock, joint author with Neil Walker of a *History of Wisbech* published in 1849. There may therefore be more than a coincidental connection between the written and photographic records. Craddock was also a photographer, and his surviving prints show him to have worked in a similar style, indeed he was probably the first of the two to do so. A man of ability, he subsequently became Professor of Literature at Queen's College, Liverpool, in which city he died, within a few months of Smith, on 9 April 1893 at the age of eighty-two.

The close connection between many of the photographs and these contemporary written records has made it possible to compare them directly in the majority of cases. Use has also been made of the *History of Wisbech* written in 1898 by F. J. Gardiner, son of and successor to the newspaper editor. It contains much nineteenth-century news in a condensed form.*

Walker & Craddock's 1849 *History* is a valuable source of description of the town at the time Smith took up photography. Many of his views of buildings might have been taken to illustrate the book.

There are, of course, photographs which cannot be compared to contemporary Wisbech sources. Most of these belong to the series of churches in the surrounding towns and villages, which are more typical of the photography of the time. But as many of the churches have since been restored, these too can provide valuable evidence for the architectural historian.

The survival or otherwise of the buildings depicted is mentioned, if at all, only in passing. Some of the views, such as North Brink (plates 57–60 etc.), are almost unchanged today; many buildings disappeared, like the Butter Cross (plates 29, 30) and Stone Bridge (plates 12, 13 etc.), in Smith's own time; others, most notably the Octagon Church (plate 61) and Old Workhouse (plate 63), have been recent and less excusable victims to ignorance and expediency; the fine tower of the eight-sail mill on Lynn Road (plate 62) has been badly damaged by fire only a few days before these words are written; the Cemetery Chapel (plate 65) has been allowed to deteriorate until all hope of saving it has gone, and within a short time it will have been demolished. As a record of vanished Wisbech the photographs are invaluable, but it is as the work of Samuel Smith, documentary photographer, that they are of much more than local significance.

* Quotations from the *Wisbech Advertiser* are indicated only by the date of the issue in which they appear.

W&C Walker & Craddock: *History of Wisbech* 1849.

G F.J. Gardiner: *History of Wisbech* 1898. Other references are given in full.

The Photography of Samuel Smith

In 1852, when Samuel Smith took up photography, the process was just thirteen years old. In 1839 details were published of two practical methods by which pictures could be made by the direct action of light on sensitive materials. The first process to be announced was the invention of the Frenchman Louis Jacques Mandé Daguerre. The Daguerreotype was made by exposing a silvered copper plate to the vapour of iodine, forming light-sensitive silver iodide on the silver surface. After exposure of many minutes in a camera, the image on the plate was developed by exposing it to the vapour from heated mercury. The mercury vapour amalgamated with the minute specks of silver formed by the action of light, making the image visible. The plate was then 'fixed' by chemical treatment to remove the remaining unused silver salts, making the image permanent. After chemical and optical improvements to the process in 1840, exposure times were reduced to around a minute, and portraiture became practical. The Daguerreotype process was soon in use throughout the world, although its use in England was restricted since Daguerre had taken a patent on the process in this country. Users had to apply for a licence to Daguerre or his agent. The Daguerreotype, used mainly for portraits, was finely detailed and could be very beautiful. However, it had several drawbacks. The materials were expensive and the manipulations complex. Each Daguerreotype was unique; copies could only be had by taking several originals or by rephotographing the image. Modern photography has evolved along a different path.

In January 1839, after hearing of Daguerre's discovery, the Englishman William Henry Fox Talbot was moved to publish the results of researches in which he had been engaged since 1834. Dissatisfied with his efforts as an amateur artist, he had begun to search for ways of recording images directly from nature. He prepared sensitive paper by first treating it with a solution of common salt, then washing it over with a solution of silver nitrate. The paper was thus impregnated with silver chloride, which darkened rapidly when exposed to light. By placing leaves, lace and other objects in contact with the paper and exposing them to light, shadow pictures of the objects could be made. These 'photogenic drawings', as Fox Talbot called them, could be 'fixed' by treating the exposed paper with a strong salt solution, which so reduced the sensitivity of the paper that the images could be viewed in subdued light. In 1835, in tiny cameras made for him by the local carpenter, Fox Talbot recorded images of his home, Lacock Abbey in Wiltshire. One of these pictures, of a lattice window, survives and is preserved in the Science Museum, London. The 'photogenic drawings' were negatives—that is to say, the tone values of the original subject were reversed in the picture—light became dark, dark, light. By 1839 Fox Talbot had found that if a negative was placed in contact with sensitive paper and exposed to light, a positive print was made, restoring the tones of the original scene. This negative-positive principle is the basis of modern photography.

Compared with the rival Daguerreotype process, 'photogenic drawing' had several drawbacks. It was much less sensitive, exposures in the camera requiring many minutes or even hours. The salt-fixed images were not very permanent, and in fineness of detail could not compare with the Daguerreotype. Fox Talbot continued to experiment, and in 1840 discovered that a brief exposure in the camera produced a 'latent' image in the paper, invisible to the eye but capable of being revealed by chemical development. By greatly amplifying the effect of light, this process reduced exposure times to a mere minute or two. Fox Talbot called his new process 'calotype' (from a Greek root meaning beautiful). Later it also became known as 'Talbotype', in his honour. The new process was patented in 1841, and although licences were readily granted for its use, it was not so widely employed for professional use as the Daguerreotype. Simpler and cheaper than its rival, the calotype process was used mainly by amateurs for landscape and architectural work; portraits are rare, except for the remarkable pictures by the Scots D. O. Hill and Robert Adamson.

As time passed several variations on the calotype process appeared. The most notable improvement was devised in 1850 by the Frenchman Gustave le Gray. It had been normal practice to impregnate the developed calotype negative with wax to make it translucent for printing. Le Gray discovered that by waxing the paper *before* sensitizing two advantages were derived. Firstly, the capacity of the paper for recording fine detail was greatly enhanced. Secondly, the keeping properties of the prepared paper were improved. It was usual to expose calotype paper soon

after preparing it, ideally while it was still moist. Waxed negative paper, on the other hand, would keep its properties for weeks or even months before use. However, the waxed paper material was less sensitive than the normal calotype paper, requiring as much as ten or fifteen minutes in the camera, but for architectural and landscape subjects, for which the process was used principally, this was no great drawback.

In 1852, when Samuel Smith decided to take up photography, there were several possibilities open to him. The Daguerreotype process was still widely used, but, at least in England, confined mainly to professional portraiture. Calotype photography and its variations were available. In 1851, a new process had been described by the sculptor and calotypist Frederick Scott Archer. In an attempt to overcome the problems of printing from a paper negative, Scott Archer devised a method of coating glass with a sensitive layer. A solution of collodion—guncotton dissolved in ether—containing suitable salts was spread on a glass plate and sensitized by immersion in a silver nitrate bath immediately before exposing. As soon as exposure was complete, the plate was developed and fixed. The need to prepare the plate just before using it required that the photographer carry a portable darktent when working away from home. Although the new process yielded glass negatives of high quality and exceptional definition, the need to carry a darktent, several chemical solutions, water, a camera and tripod and other accessories proved a deterrent to many. Perhaps for this reason, the fifty-year-old Smith decided to use the paper negative process. In May 1852, under pressure from leading photographers and with the competition of the wet collodion process, Fox Talbot relinquished his patent rights for all uses except professional portraiture. By October of that year, Smith had taken up photography; his earliest surviving negative is dated 12 October 1852 (plate 5). It is probable that he adopted the waxed paper process of Le Gray, details of which had been published in England in 1851.

To prepare his negative material, Smith first required thin, fine textured paper of a type suitable for sensitizing. In England, the two leading suppliers of such material were Whatman, of Turkey Mills, and R. Turner, of Chafford Mills. Smith appears to have

Figure 1 Watermarks from paper negatives by Smith.

favoured the latter's products; many of his negatives were made on paper bearing watermarks: R TURNER 1847, R TURNER CHAFFORD MILLS, PHOTOGRAPHIC R TURNER and R TURNER PATENT TALBOTYPE (figure 1). After rejecting any sheets with obvious impurities or irregularities, Smith would then wax the paper. An English translation of Le Gray's work *A Practical Treatise on Photography*, published by Willats in 1851, explained how this was done. After heating a carefully levelled metal plate,

. . . rub a piece of white wax over the plate, which will melt. When there is a good coating of melted wax, place your paper upon it, assisting its adherence with a card. When it has imbibed equally, withdraw it, and place it between several sheets of fine blotting paper, over which

you pass an iron moderately hot, to take up the excess
of wax. It is very essential that the wax should be very
equally taken up and that none remain but in the texture
of the paper.

The waxed paper was then iodized by soaking in a
solution of potassium iodide containing organic
materials such as rice water and sugar of milk, which
probably acted as binding agents to ensure adhesion
of the potassium iodide to the waxed paper fibres.
The dried iodized paper was then cut to size and
stored in a portfolio until required. When the paper
was to be sensitized, a solution of silver nitrate,
acidified with acetic acid, was prepared. Le Gray
described the process:

> You plunge the waxed and iodized paper completely into
> the nitrate of silver in the first trough, and leave it there
> four or five minutes, you then withdraw it and put it
> immediately in the distilled water in the second trough,
> where you leave it at least four minutes and longer if you
> wish to preserve the paper a long time before using it.
> You can prepare in the same baths ten sheets one after
> the other. At length you take the paper from the water
> and dry it between blotting paper very clean and new—
> placing it, to preserve it, between the leaves of a quire of
> the same paper, equally new and good. . . . By keeping
> paper thus prepared from the light it will preserve its
> sensibility five or six days or more before exposure. . . .
> This mode of operation is precious for travellers, since it
> dispenses with manipulations so difficult when one is
> away from home.

These operations, of course, were carried out in very
subdued light.

Among the surviving negatives by Smith are a
number which show his home, Malvern House, from
substantially the same viewpoint and taken on many
different occasions (figure 2). From their dates, it is
clear that each one was taken just before a series of
pictures of some important subject, usually after a
period of inactivity. It is probable that Smith, having
prepared a new batch of paper, tested it with a
photograph of his standard subject. By comparing
the new result with earlier negatives of known
quality, he would be able to check quickly the success
of the sensitizing operation. It is an interesting
example of Smith's methodical approach to
photography.

Smith's earliest negatives were approximately
seven and a half inches by nine and a half inches in
size, but it seems probable that in April 1859 he
acquired a new camera, for from this time on all his
negatives are slightly larger—just over eight and a

Figure 3 A calotype camera, *c.* 1850.

Figure 4 Two details showing a calotype camera in use:
    left – Croyland Abbey, 1855 (detail from plate 81);
    right – Ely Cathedral, 1854 (detail from plate 78).

half inches by ten and a half inches. We do not know what camera Smith possessed. Indeed, it is quite possible that, mechanically skilled, he made his own apparatus. However, most cameras of this time were of essentially the same design (figure 3). Two wooden boxes, one sliding within the other, formed the body of the camera. One carried the lens, the other the focusing screen and negative holder. The sensitive paper was carried in a light-tight holder, usually with a sheet of glass to keep the paper flat. After inserting the holder in the camera, a slide was withdrawn, uncovering the sensitive surface inside the camera. Since exposures could last many minutes, the camera had to be supported on a tripod. Such a camera can be seen in the middle distance of two of Smith's photographs, at Ely in 1854, and at Croyland Abbey in 1855 (figure 4).

Although Smith's camera would have been of simple design, it almost certainly had one feature not found on most of today's complex cameras. When photographing buildings, if the camera is tilted up to include the top, the result is a picture in which the parallel vertical lines of the subject converge. This distortion is avoided if the camera is kept level, and the lens is slid upwards, raising the image in the camera so as to include the top of the subject on the sensitive surface. This 'rising front' feature, commonly fitted on later cameras, was also available on some early apparatus. From the correctly rendered verticals in most of Smith's pictures, it seems his camera was so equipped. To take a picture Smith would set up his camera, align it and carefully focus his subject on the ground glass focusing screen, using a black cloth to exclude light from the screen to facilitate the operation. When ready, the ground glass screen was removed and replaced with the paper holder, and the slide was withdrawn. To take the picture, Smith removed the lens cap, waited for the necessary minutes to pass and then replaced the cap. When the protecting slide was replaced in the paper holder, the operation was complete.

The relative insensitivity of the waxed paper process made long exposure times necessary. Some of Smith's negatives have exposure times written on the edge—twelve or fifteen minutes were given to some pictures (figure 5). Many of the clock faces appearing in his pictures show blurring of the minute hands over similar periods (figure 6). Since most of Smith's

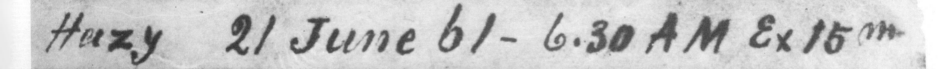

Lyra   July 2·1856

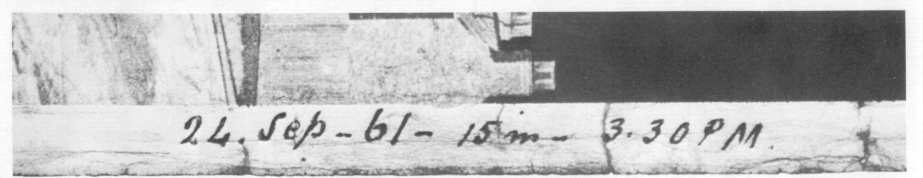

Hazy   21 June 61 - 6·30 AM Ex 15 m·

24. Sep - 61 - 15 m - 3·30 PM.

Figure 5 Dates, exposure details etc. from Smith's
negatives: *top – negative of plate 41;*
centre – negative of plate 1.

Figure 6 Two details from Smith's photographs showing
blurred minute hands, due to exposure times of from
ten to fifteen minutes: *left – detail from plate 76.*

15

Figure 7 'Self portraits' – enlarged details from Smith's photographs.

subjects were inanimate, these long times were no great drawback. Indeed, he exploited them on occasion, to enable him to appear in his own pictures. A number of his pictures show Smith, usually seated, in the foreground or middle distance (figure 8). He would remove the lens cap, move briskly into the scene and adopt his pose, remaining still until the allotted time was almost up. He would then return quickly to the camera and replace the cap.

In several pictures, the figure of Smith is slightly transparent, indicating that he was not present for the entire exposure time (figure 7). The long duration of exposure is also responsible for the fact that, in Smith's photographs, the streets of Wisbech appear to be deserted. Although, no doubt, the inhabitants of the town were about their business while the pictures were taken, only those who stayed still for much of the exposure time would be recorded. In a few photographs, such as the delightful picture of the 'condemned' shops on the Cornhill, people were persuaded by Smith to stand still for the duration (plates 23, 24). In most pictures, however, only the occasional ghostly figure of a horse and cart or passer-by can be discerned. For the same reason, Smith was careful to take most of his photographs of shipping on the River Nene at low tide. With the ships grounded, there would be no movement to blur the fine detail of rigging and masts. At high tide, the rocking of the boats would have destroyed the clarity of the photograph.

When the negatives had been taken, Smith would return home to his darkroom to develop them. Le Gray recommended a solution of gallic acid—a compound derived from nut galls:

Pour some of this solution into a shallow trough, and plunge the proof completely in it so that it shall be entirely covered on both sides. Follow its development which is easily seen through the thickness of the paper. It must be left thus from ten minutes to an hour or two, and sometimes more until it has arrived at perfection. With the waxed paper you may leave it one or two days without inconvenience, when the exposure has been very short. . . .

To fix the negative, the standard agent was 'hypo'— hyposulphite of soda—known today as sodium thiosulphate, the silver salt dissolving properties of which had been discovered by Sir John Herschel in 1819 and recommended by him for photographic fixing in 1839. The developed negative was placed in

Figure 8 Leverington Hall with a self-portrait by Smith – *enlargement inset (8 June 1853).*

Figure 9 A mounted and captioned print by Smith
(*see plate 39*).

No 4

Looking up stream. Part of the River at low water above proposed Dock.

Vessels at extreme left hand in distance show the upper end of bend of river proposed to convert into Dock.

a solution of 'hypo' until all the remaining unused silver salts had been removed, and the paper was washed then to remove all traces of chemicals, and dried. Le Gray recommended warming the dried negatives:

... they need only to be brought near to the fire, in order to give back to the wax that transparency which has been removed by the successive baths. Before this operation, they are full of spots, which need excite no alarm, for they disappear by this operation....

To make prints, the negatives were placed in contact with suitably sensitized paper (see below) in a printing frame. This device was a shallow box glazed with a sheet of plate glass at the bottom, upon which the negative was placed, image upwards. A sheet of prepared sensitive paper was placed upon it, then a back with a device of clips or screws with which sufficient pressure could be applied to bring negative and printing paper in close contact. Usually, the back was hinged in the centre to allow the progress of printing to be inspected without disturbing the registration of the negative. The printing frame was taken into strong daylight, preferably sunlight, and almost immediately the printing paper started to darken where light fell on it. Those parts of the printing paper protected by the denser parts of the negative darkened only slowly, while the areas under the almost transparent parts of the negative, where little exposure had occurred in the camera, darkened rapidly. Printing was continued until the whole print was much darker than finally required. The print was removed from the frame in the darkroom, and placed in a bath of 'hypo' to fix it. During this operation, the image became much lighter, and changed colour from a purplish black to a warm sepia. Sometimes, to improve the image colour and permanence of the print, a solution of gold chloride was added to the fixing bath. To complete the operation, the print was washed for a long period to remove the fixing chemicals, and dried. The dry print was usually mounted in an album or on mounting board (figure 9).

A few of the surviving prints made by Smith are on the 'salted' paper of the type used in the ordinary calotype process, and essentially the same as that used by Fox Talbot in his 'photogenic drawing' process of 1834. Most, however, are made on paper sensitized by a new process first described by

Louis-Desiré Blanquart-Evrard in 1850. Le Gray's book described the method:

Take white of eggs, to which add the fifth part, by volume, of saturated solution of chloride of sodium ... then beat it into a froth, and decant the clear liquid after it has settled for one night. Pour out the liquid into a basin, and prepare your positive paper on one side only.

This was done by floating the paper carefully on the surface of the albumen—white of egg.

Hang it up by the corner to dry.... Place your sheets (thus prepared and dried) one on the other between two leaves of white paper, and pass over them several times a very hot iron, taking out a leaf each time; you will thus render the albumen insoluble. The iron should be as hot as it can be without scorching the paper.... The paper thus prepared is very highly varnished. If you desire to obtain less gloss, add, before beating the eggs, the half or more of distilled water ... you may thus modify at pleasure the degree of brilliancy of the proof.... You may keep this paper some time before you apply the nitrate of silver to it, as it does not spoil. When you desire to use it, put the albumen side on a bath of nitrate of silver ... and let it imbibe four or five minutes, then hang it by the corner to dry.

Unlike the matt 'salted paper' prints, albumen prints had a fine lustre, almost a gloss, and were much more detailed owing to the smooth surface produced. In addition, albumen prints showed less tendency to fading than those made by the earlier method. Even so, inadequate fixing and washing have caused deterioration in the prints of many of Smith's contemporaries. By contrast, virtually all Smith's pictures are still in good condition, further testimony to his methodical habits. Fortunately for us, Smith's orderly mind led him to date most of his negatives (figure 5). On the edge of the negative, usually in the lower righthand corner, he wrote in ink the day, month and year. Most of Smith's photographs were made between April and September each year, June being the most popular month. Since bright light conditions were needed for manageably short exposure times, this was to be expected. Some negatives carry additional information—location, time of day, exposure times, ships' names and, occasionally, details of variations in the process used. Many negatives have the sky areas painted over with opaque red or black ink (figure 10). In early negatives, skies showed no details of clouds since the sensitive material responded equally to the blue and white light coming from the sky and clouds. In addition, the

Figure 10 Waxed paper negatives by Smith with sky blocked out with black ink: *top – subject as plate 71 (right) but taken nine years later; bottom – plate 76.*

Figure 11 Panorama made up of two prints taken from the
same viewpoint (*see plate 71*).

long exposures of the waxed paper process would not
have permitted the recording of moving clouds. In
printing, the effect of the paper grain was most
obvious in areas of even tone, and mottle was often
apparent in sky areas on the print. To avoid this,
photographers often painted out the skies on the
negative with opaque medium, producing featureless
white areas in the print. To relieve this effect,
sometimes clouds were printed in from another
negative in a second printing operation (plate 73).
Among prints by Smith are a number where this
technique of double printing has been used, including
some examples where prints from the same negative
have been made with and without added clouds.

We cannot say just what proportion of Smith's total
output is represented by the almost four hundred
photographs which still survive, but it must be a large
one. He worked with the paper negative process from

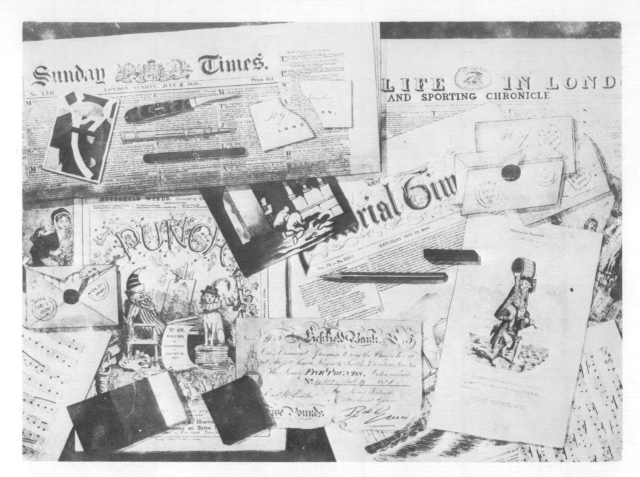

1852 to 1864 (his last dated negative was made on 24 May 1864). He was one of the last calotype photographers. There is no evidence that he ever tried the wet collodion glass plate process, which had been adopted by most of his contemporaries. It would have had few advantages for him, since he seems to have been principally interested in architectural photography, and appears never to have tried portraiture. The only exceptions among his negatives are a small number of copies of paintings, maps and engravings, showing the remarkable capacity of the waxed paper negative process for recording fine detail (figure 12). The paper processes have often been adversely compared to the Daguerreotype and wet collodion processes in this respect, but Smith's photographs are extraordinarily detailed.

Smith appears to have given up active photography in 1864, perhaps because of advancing years (he was sixty-two), but more probably because he had achieved his aim of recording his home town and its environs. Perhaps he wanted to spend more time on his many other interests. He continued to make prints from his negatives, and it is likely that the prints in the presentation album in the Wisbech and Fenland Museum were made many years later. Some show blurring of the image due to movement of the negative during printing. Since Smith's technical standards were usually high, it is probable that these prints were made when, in later life, his eyesight was poor and he was unable to detect the fault.

Samuel Smith has emerged as a figure of significance in the early history of photography. He had no influence on the development of photography, making no technical improvements to the process, and seems to have had no contact with photographers outside Wisbech. However, through his use of photography systematically to record his home town he pioneered techniques which did not come into general use for many years. The high technical and aesthetic quality of much of his work entitles him to comparison with many of his better-known contemporaries. His use of 'before and after' comparisons is all the more effective for the care that he took to match up the two records. He would have carried a copy of his earlier photograph with him so as to be able to match the new image on the focusing screen. His attention to detail in dating and identifying his pictures make them especially valuable as historic documents.

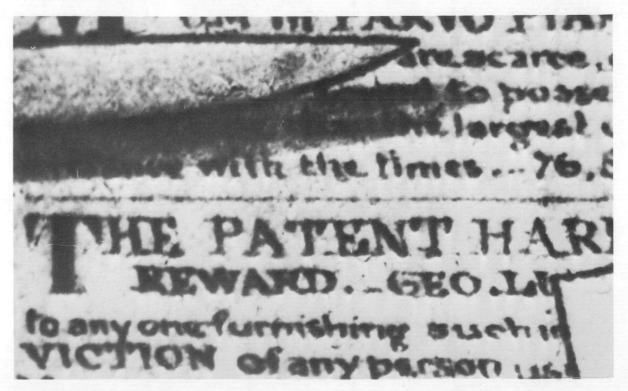

Figures 13, 14 Photographers' advertisements in the
Wisbech Advertiser, September 1855.

Other Wisbech photographers
There were a few professional photographers working
in Wisbech during Smith's period of activity. The
local newspaper carried from time to time
advertisements of itinerant photographers who set up
business for a few weeks at a time in rented premises.
In particular, in the early 1850's, Mr Sarony and

Mr D. Groom (figure 13) visited the town several
times, advertising a range of photographic services.
The introduction of the wet collodion process in 1851,
free from any restrictions of patents, made possible a
cheap method of portraiture. A whitened collodion
negative image was backed with black lacquer or
velvet, thus reflecting as a positive image. These

MR. D. GROOM'S
PHOTOGRAPHIC PORTRAIT ROOMS,
At Mr. Wade's, Boot and Shoe-Maker, High Street,
WISBECH,
WILL REMAIN OPEN FOR A SHORT TIME ONLY.

THE wide difference and superiority of Mr. G's. system over the old ones will be at once perceived; the beauty of the colouring, and the ease and freedom of the figure, render the contrast striking when compared. The extraordinary low rates of these Pictures, from 2s. upwards, place them within the reach of all.

Specimens may be seen at the Rooms, High Street.——Business Hours from Ten to Four.

PHOTOGRAPHIC PORTRAITS
TAKEN in a FEW SECONDS, by R. PARKER, Hair Dresser, High Street, in Frame complete, One Shilling.

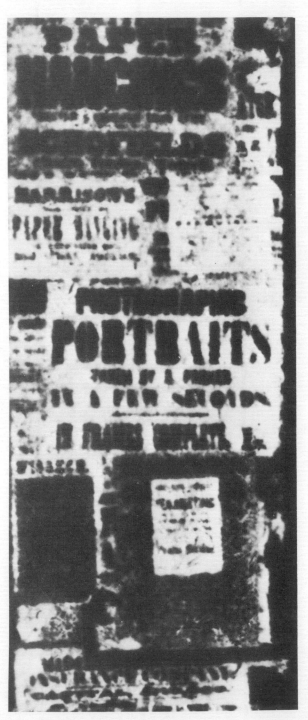

Figure 16 Parker's High Street shop, 1854;
detail from plate 50.

Figure 15 R. Parker's poster on the Butter Cross, 1856;
detail from plate 30.

Figure 17 Smith's companion, probably Thomas Craddock; *detail from plate 6.*

'collodion positives', or 'Ambrotypes' as they were sometimes known, were very much cheaper to produce than the Daguerreotype, although generally inferior in quality. The necessary modicum of skill and equipment needed were easily come by, and portrait photography was taken up by many proprietors of coffee shops, butchers, tobacconists and the like. Such a one was 'Professor' Parker, a hairdresser of the High Street, Wisbech (plate 50, figure 16). In 1855 he began to advertise in the local newspaper his portraits 'Taken in a few seconds. In Frame complete, One Shilling.' (figure 14). In one of Smith's photographs of the Butter Cross, taken in 1856, one of Parker's posters can be seen pasted up (plate 30, figure 15). From the 1860's, a number of professional portrait photographers opened up businesses in Wisbech. One, E. Johnson, photographed Smith in later life.

The most notable of Smith's contemporaries was the calotypist Thomas Craddock. As we have seen, Craddock was an acquaintance of Smith's and may well have instructed him in photography, in which he was already experienced, having exhibited photographs at the Great Exhibition in 1851. The calotype camera to be seen in two of Smith's pictures (figure 4, plates 78, 81) is probably that of Craddock, who may be the top-hatted figure seen in another of the Croyland Abbey photographs (plate 80). The same figure appears, with Smith or alone, in other photographs, notably in one taken in Leverington in April 1853 (plate 6). The elegant top-hatted gentleman seated before the camera, carrying a brass lens or lens cap, is almost certainly Craddock (figure 17). Confirmation of the relationship between the two calotypists is given by the presence of Smith in one of Craddock's photographs preserved in the Wisbech and Fenland Museum. By happy coincidence, a photograph is preserved in an album in Peckover House, Wisbech, which is almost certainly that taken by the camera shown in Smith's photograph at Croyland Abbey. The local newspaper reported in 1854 that Prince Albert had requested a copy of a calotype taken by Craddock of Ely Cathedral and exhibited in London. Since this was most likely the picture taken with the camera visible in Smith's photograph of Ely, an attempt was made to trace the picture in the Royal Collection at Windsor. Unfortunately, it does not seem to have survived; so far, a search of the Royal archives has not brought it to light.

The Townscapes

1 Leverington Village. *21 June 1861*.

Leverington

2 **Leverington House.**
Built in about 1852, it incorporates, among other architectural fragments, part of the Octagon Church lantern which was taken down in 1846 (cf. plate 61). May 1853.

Leverington is a substantial village north of Wisbech. Malvern House, Leverington Terrace, Smith's home for over forty years, lies away from the centre of the village near the banks of the Nene at Horseshoe Corner, where it can still be recognized from his many photographs.

His landlord was Thomas Peatling, a local brewer and wine merchant, who in about 1852 built a new house

3 Leverington House: the grotto. *26 June 1857.*

just to the west of Leverington Terrace. Almost a Gothic folly, it incorporates fragments of older buildings, including parts of the lantern of the Octagon Church, Wisbech, built in 1826. The house still stands with only minor alterations, but most of the stonework which lay about the garden has disappeared, as has the grotto, of which no trace can now be found.

At the other end of the terrace, on the river side,

4 Leverington: Robert Reid's steam flour mill, Horseshoe
Corner. *8 June 1858.*

stood the recently built Horseshoe Steam Mill,
illustrating a different aspect of the Victorian age.
This fine building was then used as a flour mill by
Robert Reid of Wisbech, who also ran a brewery. The
mill later became a sweet factory and then a food
processing plant. It burnt down in about 1930, but
parts of it can still be seen in the untidy warehouse
which now occupies the site.

5 Leverington: the rear of Leverington Hall.
Smith's earliest dated photograph. 12 October 1852.

Smith's earliest dated photograph was taken near the centre of Leverington. It shows farm buildings and the rear of Leverington Hall, the most important house in the village (which, in 1927, came into the hands of the Peatling family, who moved there from Leverington House). A photograph taken a few months later shows the house from the front, still much as it is today except for a new porch.

6 Leverington Hall.
The figure sitting on the fence is almost certainly Thomas Craddock, Smith's friend and fellow photographer. He appears to be holding a lens cap. 28 April 1853.

This photograph is enhanced by the presence of a figure sitting on the fence. Figures are rare in Smith's photography because of the long exposure times, but in this instance it seems certain the man is Thomas Craddock, Smith's friend and fellow photographer.

Walker & Craddock's *History of Wisbech* says of the village church:

Leverington possesses one of the most beautiful churches

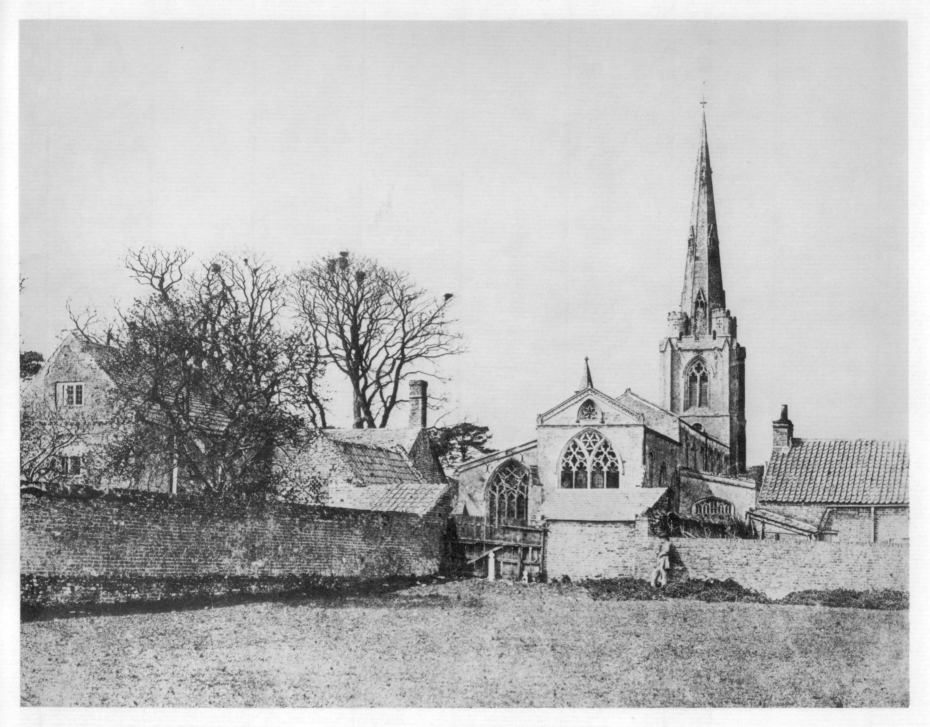

7 Leverington: St Leonard's Church from the east, *with an unidentified figure leaning on the wall. 18 May 1855.*

in a district abounding with beautiful churches. . . . The prevalent style is Perpendicular, though there are elegant examples of the Early English in the tower and of Decorated at the east end. . . . The tower and spire is the triumph of this edifice, and wherever seen, as a landmark over the wide fen, or half hidden in its surrounding trees, it is always a pleasing object, the thin spire, beautifully diminished, almost melting into the sky of which it seems to form a part. . . .

On the south side of the church is one of the most

remarkable features—a fine porch of the Decorated period. . . . Over the entrance is a small pinnacled and crocketted window, with a niche of similar character over it. This window lights a small parvise, now disused, and sadly deformed with rubbish.
(W&C, *pp. 503–5*)

Although the church was extensively restored in the nineteenth century and the spire rebuilt in 1901, it has changed very little in external appearance.

8 Leverington:
   St Leonard's Church, west end.
   28 April 1853

9 Leverington:
St Leonard's Church, south porch.
29 July 1857

10 Leverington: the eighteenth-century Rectory.
   28 August 1854.

11 Leverington: an excavation into the Rabbit Hill, a
tumulus of uncertain origin.
*No record of this excavation has been found, but the
photograph illustrates Smith's archaeological interests.
6 April 1859.*

It is pleasant to be able to visit Smith's adopted
village and see the house in which he lived and worked,
surrounded by most of the buildings he photographed,
still in existence well over a hundred years later. But
had his photographs all been of this sort, they would
be little more than good, early views of rural
Cambridgeshire. It is his documentation of change in
nearby Wisbech which is of special interest.

Introduction

Wisbech, an ancient borough and self-styled 'Capital of the Fens', stands astride the Nene at the northern end of the Isle of Ely, close to its borders with Norfolk and Lincolnshire. It is still a market town and river port as it was in 1850, and the great fertility of the surrounding countryside has made it an important agricultural centre.

In 1853, it could be said that Wisbech—

is one of the most considerable and thriving towns in the Isle of Ely and Cambridgeshire, and consists of the parish of Wisbeach St. Peter, with 6,450 acres, and a population in 1851, of 10,178. Wisbeach is in the Hundred of the same name and Liberty of the Isle of Ely, on the borders of Norfolk, within a few miles of the sea, to which it has access by the navigable river Nene and which makes it a port. By the Wisbeach Canal it has also a continuous communication by the Ouse with Cambridge, Hertford and London. This town is 87 miles from London north, 25 miles north of Ely, 40 north of Cambridge. It is the seat of the January and July quarter sessions for the Liberty of the Isle of Ely, a polling place for the shire, a market and union town, railway station, and the seat of the petty sessions for the Hundred. Here is a fine and large church. The Union Workhouse is capable of containing 600 inmates and averages 300 inmates. There is a House of Correction for the Isle of Ely and Borough of Wisbech: average number of prisoners is 43. Here is a custom-house with a collector and controller and a small establishment. The town is governed by a municipal corporation, and is formed into two wards, north ward and south ward, with a mayor, 6 aldermen, 18 town councillors, a separate commission of the peace, a treasurer, town clerk, town chamberlain; charitable trustees, harbour master, superintendent of police, &c. The town is lighted with gas, and there is an exchange hall and council rooms, a sessions house, a stamp office under a sub-distributor, a museum, newsroom, literary society and library, &c. Besides the parish Church of St. Peter, the living of which constitutes a vicarage, of which the Rev. Henry Fardell is incumbent, with two curates; there is a chapel of ease in the Old Market; also a Roman Catholic Chapel, and Chapels for Baptists 2, Independants, Unitarians, Wesleyans and two other Dissenting Sects, and a Friends Meeting House. There is a Grammar School, a National School for boys and girls, a British School for boys and girls, an Infant School, banks, a savings bank, a newspaper, cemetery for Churchmen, and another for Dissenters. The chief trade is in shipping, corn, potatoes, bones, wool, seeds, hides, coal, timber &c, and in the building and repair of ships, boats and barges. There are also machine works and three foundries, reel cotton manufactory, brickfields, breweries, rope works, cooperage, printing office, tannery, mast and block works, corn mills, tobacco-pipe works, &c. In the year ending September 1st 1845, 250,000 quarters of corn were sold at Wisbeach, which is one of the largest markets in England. Vessels of 400 tons enter the port, steamers run to Hull, and 132,814 tons of shipping cleared in and out in the course of the year 1851. The market day is Saturday, when sometimes 9,000 quarters of wheat have been sold. The fair days are Wednesday before Whit Sunday, and July 25th, for horses, and August 12th for beasts. There is now railway communication hence to all parts of England, which has somewhat injured the shipping trade of this port. (*Introduction to the Wisbech Section of the 1853 Post Office directory*)

The River

Despite much earlier origins, Wisbech, even today, has the appearance of a Georgian town. The photographs by Samuel Smith of the Brinks seen through the arch of the old bridge must be among the most evocative pictures of Georgian architecture in existence.

Only a few months after these photographs were taken, the bridge had gone, a casualty of the extensive river works intended to improve the navigation and drainage of the Nene over much of its course.

The story of the Nene Valley Improvements is an interesting and instructive tale. The newspaper accounts of the period began with fears for the town because of the dangerous state of the bridge and river, and welcomed the news that something was to be done. As the works progressed at enormous expense hope became tinged with regret and then dismay. The final scenes were of bitter confrontation between the town and the Nene Valley Commissioners.

While there does seem to be a remarkable coincidence between Smith's photographic career and the period of the river works, his home was near the river bank, from which many of his photographs are taken, and he can be expected to have had an interest in shipping.

The Nene's importance is not just as a navigable channel to the sea, but as the main drain for a wide area, which the particular problems of Fenland geography make very susceptible to small changes. In addition, it was at that time essential for the supply of water and disposal of sewage in the town. The state of the river was a subject of general concern on which the prosperity of Wisbech depended more than it does now.

Wisbech interests put almost all the blame for the decline of the port and town during the 1850's on to the river works. While there can be little doubt that these did adversely affect the port, tonnages were already falling before the works began. The railways affected the coastal trade markedly, and, in any case, the port was too small for many of the ever larger ships to use.

The Nene Valley Drainage Act was passed in 1852 to put into effect the proposals of James Rendel that the river bank at Wisbech be piled and stoned, the river dredged to a uniform depth, the worst bends removed, shoals taken away and the bridge at Wisbech replaced so as not to restrict the current. The cost was to be £150,000, of which Wisbech was to contribute £40,000 and the proceeds of a halfpenny tonnage due levied on shipping, estimated to produce annually £177 or, if capitalized at twenty years' purchase, £3,540.

The corporation at first strongly opposed the measures, but trusting to the clauses of the act and their distinguished consultant engineer, Robert Stephenson, they withdrew their opposition.

The Admiralty wanted an opening bridge so that navigation could be established to Peterborough. This was opposed by the town, the main objections, apart from cost, being first that there was no proof large vessels could get up to Peterborough even if an opening bridge was provided, and also the inconvenience which would be caused. To illustrate the second point a survey was taken in May 1852 of all traffic across the stone bridge:

Traffic over	Persons	Horses	Carriages	Cattle	Total
Thurs. 20 May	9,060	617	418	590	10,685
Fri. 21 May	7,620	401	274	99	8,394
Sat. 22 May	21,460	693	529	1,071	23,753
Sun. 23 May	8,770	104	64	213	9,151
Mon. 24 May	10,590	704	432	689	12,415
Tues. 25 May	8,680	522	650	144	9,696
Wed. 26 May	7,580	628	369	444	9,021

(*June 1852*)

12 Wisbech: the North Brink through the arch of the Stone Bridge.
The damage to the bank caused by the floods of November 1852 can be seen under the arch, on the right. The old Friends' Meeting House (see page 90) is the low building with two dormer windows on the left next to the house with 'Jacobean' gables (cf. plates 57 and 58). 17 June 1853.

In November 1852, heavy rains dramatically affected the amount of water in the Nene, causing a great torrent through the narrow channel and sharp curve by the bridge. The wing wall of the north-west side of the bridge gave way, taking with it some of the road. Chalk was thrown into the breach to prevent collapse of the bridge, and just downstream, buildings behind Cornhill were carried away and part of Nene Quay

collapsed. The damage continued for days making evacuation of riverside homes necessary.

The Nene Valley Commissioners were asked if their plans were sufficient, but six months later—

The Bridge, the wing wall of which was carried away last November, is in a very doubtful state of security, the foundations having within the last few days been found to be undermined by the action of the water to the extent

13 Wisbech: the Brinks and the Stone Bridge.
The Friends' Meeting House has been rebuilt.
4 September 1854.

of nine feet; stones have been put into the hole to prevent, if possible, any further scour, but . . . very little dependence ought to be placed on its stability. It has long been a great impediment to traffic and, if it could be carried away without injury to anyone, its departure would be little regretted.
(*May 1853*)

In July, dismay was expressed that the work had not started, despite payment of a third of the £40,000

Wisbech was to contribute towards the cost. By September, things had begun to move:

The occupiers of property in the vicinity of the bridge, from the post office to the King's Head, and also some on the opposite side of the river, have received notices that their premises will be required, and requesting them to deliver their claims for compensation within 21 days. The contracts for the works have been advertised, and the tenders will be decided upon, it is supposed, almost

14 Wisbech: A steam pump on the river bank,
opposite the Canal outlet. No date.

15 Wisbech: the Royal Sailor, Nene Parade,
*with the steam engine and pile driver. No date (c. early
1854).*

immediately. Everybody, except perhaps some of the
residents on the spot, will be gratified to see the
improvement carried forward forthwith.
(*September 1853*)

And a few months later, in February 1854, the first
pile for the erection of a stage to hold the pile driving
machine was driven in just above the entrance to the
Canal, and piles were driven in lower down the bank.

The banks of the river present a busy appearance with
the preparations now going forward for the permanent
works. A small steam engine has been erected in Nene
Parade, another is in course of erection on the opposite
side, for the purpose of driving the piles, and it is
anticipated that the progress of the works will shortly be
very rapid.
(*April 1854*)

On Friday 21 April—

16 Wisbech: Nene Quay and the warehouses behind the Old Market, just below the bridge.
Pile driving is proceeding on both banks and the steam engine is in position behind the King's Head. No date (c. late 1854).

the first permanent pile of the river works was driven into the Eastfield bank. A small steam engine has been for some time erected opposite the 'Royal Sailor' on the Nene Parade and the pile driving machines are worked by its agency, a great saving of human labour being the result, as well as greater rapidity in the execution of the works. Several machines are worked at once, the 'monkey' which in the largest machine weighs 1¾ tons, being raised in a few seconds. The road along the Nene Quay is now stopped by piling machines, which have

17 Wisbech: Nene Quay, at about the same time as
plate 16.
*The improvement which took place in the Quay can be seen
in plate 31. No date (c. late 1854).*

been driving piles in the road in front and at each side of
Mr. Harrison's granary at the corner of New Inn Yard
for the purpose of keeping up the wharf, which had very
nearly found its way into the river.
(*May 1854*)

The engine was later moved to the bank behind the
King's Head, where it appears on another photograph;
in February 1856, the *Advertiser* reported that 'A
quantity of lead pipe has been stolen from the small

18 Wisbech: the river Nene.
Boucher's brewery, Nene Parade, is on the left. The Old Workhouse, Albion Place, can be seen in the middle background behind the Canal outfall. Pile driving is in progress on the bank to the right. No date (c. 1854).

steam engine belonging to Mr Leather, by the river side, near the King's Head.'

By late summer of 1854, concern was being expressed at the state of the works, and from then on, discontent with the progress becomes far more common.

It is very desirable that the footpath on the Nene Parade should be restored as soon as practicable, as accidents are very liable to happen by persons falling into the space

19 Wisbech: the river Nene,
*showing the progress of the river works. A 'before and
after' pair with plate 18. No date (c. 1855–6).*

between the bank and the front row of piling. An instance
occurred on Monday night, 24 July, when the locality
being rather crowded, a young man named Limer fell in
among the iron ties and piles, and although he fortunately
suffered no bodily hurt, his clothes were much bemired.
(*August 1854*)

In June 1854 a dredger, probably the machine in the
photograph, was lying in the river ready for action. It
was destroyed on 9 November 1855, when—

20 Wisbech: the steam engine, *in position opposite Nene Quay (cf. plate 16). No date (c. 1854–5).*

21 The Nene below Wisbech, with the dredging machine. *The paddle-tug is probably the 'Don', owned by Richard Young. This photograph and plates 36 and 37 were taken from the river bank close to Smith's home in Leverington Terrace. No date (c. 1854).*

. . . a fire was discovered on board the large dredging machine which was lying in the river near the Leverington Road toll bar. Mr. Superintendent Rust and most of the police force were soon on the spot, and the fire engine under the care of Mr. Jennings attended immediately with part of the fire brigade. The dredging machine was in flames, and notwithstanding the utmost efforts of all who were present to subdue the fire, the vessel was greatly injured.
(*16 November 1855*)

A replacement was soon built, which remained in the Nene until 1858, when—

The dredging machine, which has acted an important if not a useful part in the river works, was brought down the river at three o'clock on Saturday morning, at low water to enable it to pass under the bridges, and was conveyed away by two steam tugs from Hull to some place in that vicinity.
(*1 October 1858*)

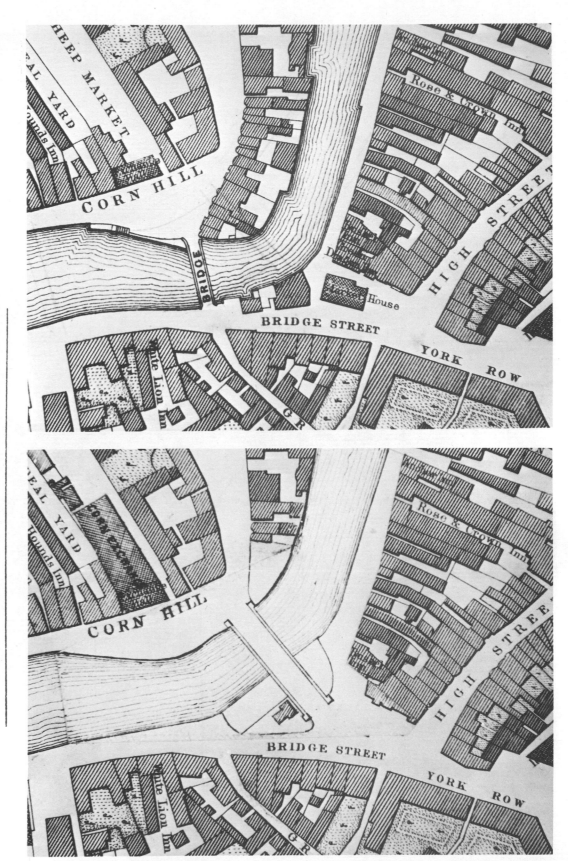

Figure 19 Details from contemporary maps of Wisbech.
*On the plan at the top are shown the old Stone Bridge with,
in faint pencil, the lines of the proposed new Iron Bridge
and, on the extreme left, of the temporary wooden bridge.
The lower plan shows the Iron Bridge in place and the
houses in Cornhill (see plates 22–25) and Bridge Street (see
plates 29–30) now demolished, including the Butter Cross
('Market House'). Note too the new Corn Exchange in the
former Sheep Market (see plates 57–8). Both details are
from F. J. Utting's map of 1850 (see end papers), the
alterations in the lower one having been made in 1859.*

BUILDING MATERIALS.

TO BE SOLD BY AUCTION, BY

MR. GEORGE JAMES MARSHALL,

On MONDAY, the 16th day of June inst., under the
direction of the Nene Valley Drainage and Navigation Improvement Commissioners,

ALL the MATERIALS of the BUILDING situate
in Wisbech, and used as the Poultry Market,
Magistrates' Rooms, Police and other Offices, consisting
of a large quantity of Lead, Slates, Freestone, York-
shire Flag Stones, Fir Timber of Roof, Floors and
Joists, Staircases, Doors, Frames, Windows, Shutters,
Wainscotting, Closet Fronts and Doors, Chimney
Pieces, Water Closet Seat and Apparatus, Two Large
Cast Iron Columns, Wrought Iron Gates, Palisading
and other Materials, which will be divided into Lots.

The above Materials are of the best description, and
may be viewed after the 9th inst.

The Sale to commence in the Building precisely at
Two o'clock in the Afternoon.

All Materials and Rubbish will be required to be
removed before the 1st of July next, and if any of the
Materials are not taken away before that day they will
belong to the Commissioners.

Wisbech, June 3rd, 1856.

Figure 18 Notice of sale of building materials of the
Butter Cross by order of the Commissioners
(*see pp. 57–9*).

22 Wisbech: the Stone Bridge and, on the right, the backs of the Cornhill properties demolished during the river works. *No date* (c. 1854).

In June, the Corporation sold the Butter Cross to the Commissioners, and in July—

some of the occupiers of property in Cornhill completed their arrangements with the Commissioners for compensation for removal. It is intended to remove the Post Office to the house lately occupied by Mr. Hole, surgeon, on the South Brink.
(*July 1854*)

23 Wisbech: Cornhill, looking into the Old Market.
The shops include McNeil's confectionery, Goode the
saddler and Barley the chemist. Barley moved to the
Market Place after the demolition of these premises (see
plate 52). Ford's ironmongery on the left survived the river
works but has been demolished since. 6 September 1854.

The shopkeepers of the condemned property then
began to move out. H. C. Lee, boot and shoe maker,
moved to Upper Hill Street. James Eyres, proprietor
of the 'noted tea house, drapery mart and family
grocery warehouse', moved to the other side of the
Old Market. Mr Bellars moved his drapery
establishment to the High Street. Demolition followed
swiftly:

24 Wisbech: Cornhill. *The shops continue on from the previous plate. They include Foster's drapery, holding a 'selling out' sale (he later took a shop in the Market Place, see plate 52), Bellars' grocery, Baxter's chemist and the Post Office. Mr Goward, the Post Master, is probably one of the two men standing in the doorway on the right. 6 September 1854.*

NELSON FOSTER,

No. 4, CORN HILL, WISBECH,

BEGS respectfully to inform his patrons that, in consequence of not having succeeded in procuring Premises suitable for carrying on his Business in its several Branches, he intends offering at once the WHOLE of his STOCK at such prices as will defy competition.

The STOCK consists of BROAD CLOTHS, BEAVERS, PILOTS, DOESKINS, READY-MADE CLOTHES, HATS & CAPS, also IRISHES, CALICOES, PRINTS, COBOURGS, DELAINES, &c.

☞ OPEN at 9, CLOSE at 7.

25 Wisbech: the Stone Bridge.
The damage to the bank caused by the floods of November 1852 can be seen on the left. The photograph shows buildings on both sides of the river which were demolished to make way for the new bridge. 7 June 1853.

The temporary bridge, opposite the White Hart, is now nearly completed and the demolition of the old bridge will doubtless soon follow. The line of the river through the space lately occupied by the houses in the Cornhill is marked out, and preparations are in progress for driving the permanent piles there.
(*November 1854*)

The temporary bridge was completed before the end of 1854, but the old bridge remained in use for some

time, and it was not until 22 March 1855 that—

the remains of the arch of the old bridge were let down into the river. The upper portion of the structure had been previously removed, and as much of the stonework of the arch as appeared practical without endangering its fall. A mass of about 100 tons remained, and at about 5 o'clock in the evening of the above day the workmen began to break the blocks of stone at the spring of the arch on the north side. . . . After pounding at the stones

26 Wisbech: North Brink during construction of the temporary bridge.
The view is very similar to that seen under the old bridge in plate 12. No date (c. late 1854).

until 8 o'clock, the mass of masonry fell into the river without occasioning any accident. . . . By the end of the present week, scarcely a vestige of the old bridge will remain to mark the spot where it had stood for almost a century past.

It was founded in 1758. The *Cambridge Chronicle* says 'It was a work of no small magnitude at the time of its erection, when the population of the town was not more than one sixth of its present amount and the cultivated land of the neighbourhood not in greater proportion. . . .

The plan and elevation were submitted to Mr. (afterwards Sir James) Burrough, Master of Caius College, Cambridge, who approved of the same, and a contract was entered into for £1,700 and the old bricks. Subsequently £500 more was raised and the work was completed. It may easily be imagined what the traffic then was, when a ferry opposite the White Hart Inn supplied the place of the bridge during its erection. The first stone was laid in 1758, on which was a plate with the following:

27 Wisbech: the Stone Bridge undergoing demolition.
This negative is dated 29 March, but if the newspaper
accounts are correct, it must have been taken on or before
22 March 1855.

Ex Ligneo
Surrexit Lapideus
A.D. 1758
Esto Perpetuus
We trust we shall have to record that it is deposited in
the Museum.
(*April 1855*)

In August hopes were expressed that the works would
be finished, except for the bridge, by the end of

September, but were followed early in 1856 by dismay
that, contrary to the terms of the act, works were
progressing upstream before completion of those at
Wisbech. The river was said to be worse than before
the works began.

The foundation stone of the new bridge was laid by
the Mayor on 11 April 1856, followed by a dinner and
great celebrations. It was to be—

28 Wisbech: the temporary bridge, *with the Iron Bridge under construction in the background after demolition of the buildings seen in plate 25. 17 September 1856.*

the largest opening bridge in the world; the length being 156 feet, the width 40 feet and the sides 8 feet high. The bridge will be balanced on a pivot placed at one third of its length. The shorter end will be provided with rollers and will be weighted to the extent of about 120 tons to maintain its equilibrium. The pivot is to be of a peculiar construction, the agency of water being employed after the manner of an hydraulic press: that is, the moveable part of the bridge will rest on a large piston, fitting watertight into a cylinder, into which, when it is necessary

to open the bridge, water will be pumped so as to raise the superincumbent mass and enable it to be turned with ease. When the bridge is closed and at rest the water may be let out and the bridge will repose on its usual bearings. The cost of the bridge (exclusive of the property purchased for the approaches) will be about £13,000. (*25 April 1856*)

And in June—
the sale of the materials of the building occupied as a

29 Wisbech: the Butter Cross and Justices' Rooms,
*once the Custom House also, with other buildings in Bridge
Street which were demolished during the river works.
20 September 1853.*

police station, justices' room and butter market, and
formerly the custom house, took place by auction. After
a brisk competition, the various lots realised together the
sum of £219. 19s. The lead upon the roof was the most
important lot, and realised £93 . . . . The work of
demolition commenced on Tuesday morning [17 June]
and in a few days scarcely a vestige of the building will
remain in its original position. Its removal will create a
fine opening for the adjacent property, and we have no
doubt will ultimately increase its value. Some unsightly

premises will become prominent, but their improvement
must inevitably follow.

The building, we find by Messrs. Walker and Craddock's
valuable History of Wisbech, was erected in 1801, on the
site of the old Cross and Custom House. This cross was
used for the sale of butter, of which great quantities were
sold at Wisbech. The following extracts from the
Corporation records relate to the erection of the building
now undergoing demolition, and for which we are
indebted to Mr. Craddock:—

30 Wisbech: the Butter Cross just before demolition.
*The other buildings on the site, which can be seen in plate
29, have already gone, revealing part of North Brink in
the background. One of the posters (detail, figure 15)
advertises photographic portraits by Parker, whose shop
can be seen in plate 50. 11 June 1856.*

'*Feb 3 1801—ordered, that the Town Bailiff be hereby
empowered to employ proper persons to take down the
Cross and Custom House, as soon as the same shall be
quitted by the present tenants, in a careful manner, so as to
preserve the materials for the purpose of being worked in the
erection of a new cross and building.*'

'*June 26 1801—ordered, that the plan delivered this day by
Mr. Thomas West for building a new Custom House on the
site of a spot where the old Custom House lately stood, is
approved of by the Corporation; and that the building of the
same, agreeable to the said plan, be immediately proceeded in,*

*under the direction of the Town Bailiff and the
superintendence of the said Thomas West.*'

'*Nov 10 1802—Resolved, that a further sum of one
thousand pounds be borrowed and taken up in annuities or
bonds, as soon as may be, for the purpose of paying the
tradesmen's bills incurred in the rebuilding of the Cross, and
repairing the wharfing, etc.*'

A pamphlet published by J. White, Wisbech, 1809, states
that the building was completed in 1804 by the
Corporation at a cost of £2,500.
(20 June 1856)

31 Wisbech: the 'Throttle' just below the bridge.
The improvement in Nene Quay can be seen in comparison with plate 17. No date (c. May 1857; possibly one of the series intended for the Parliamentary Committee).

However, the progress of the new bridge—

cannot be said to develop any beauty in its design, a less ornamental affair than it is likely to become it would be scarcely possible to devise.
(*25 July 1856*)

Hopes that the bridge would be speedily finished faded with the summer, and difficulties arose with the hydraulic machinery.

If the contractors do not look sharper than the frost, it will remain a fixture for winter and serve only as a glaciarium for merry and high spirited juveniles.
(*5 December 1856*)

We thought that our new bridge would be worked on purely teetotal principles, the hydraulic power being free from the touch of the 'demon spirit'. We find, however, that we were mistaken, for on asking 'our own' philosopher [surely a reference to Smith] how the bridge would be

32 Wisbech: The Iron Bridge nearing completion.
29 May 1857 (probably one of the photographs used in the
Parliamentary proceedings).

prevented from being set fast in frosty weather, he gave us to understand that this could only be prevented by diluting the water with gin, brandy, or some other alcoholic spirit which would not freeze in the temperature of our winters. The bridge was certainly considered ugly enough before, but all decent people must feel great contempt for it, when they find it can only be put in motion (at this time of year at least) when it is under the influence of liquor. We should not like to be responsible for any damage it may occasion while it is being opened or

shut in that state. Affairs are indeed come to a pretty pass in Wisbech, with 'gingerbread' engineering, and gin-and-water machinery.
(*5 December 1856*)

At the meeting of the Nene Valley Investigation Committee, it was stated, as one of the latest discoveries of the eminent scientific engineers connected with the river works, that the tail of the bridge would not be of sufficient weight to balance the larger portion, and that if

33 Wisbech: Nene Parade *after completion of the piling and erection of English's timber crane. (cf. plates 18 and 19). No date (late 1856 or after).*

swung round, it would ignominiously fall headforemost into the river.
(*27 February 1857*)

The state of Nene Parade had also been a source of constant complaint, but no sooner had the road been made up than it was obstructed by—

A very formidable looking affair in course of construction in front of Messrs. English's timber yard on the Nene Parade, as a travelling crane for landing timber over the bank in lieu of drawing it up the bank by horsepower, as has hitherto been done.
(*8 August 1856*)

Meanwhile, to solve their financial difficulties, the Commissioners went to Parliament with another Nene Valley Bill, to raise more money. Progress was slow, for a number of reasons.

34 Wisbech: the Iron Bridge,
newly painted and with stone piers complete. 13 May 1859.

At a meeting of the Commissioners at Peterborough on 6 March 1857—

it was stated that Mr. Stephenson was still in Egypt, and that Mr. Fowler had sailed for Cairo, and, in order to ensure their presence, the meeting was adjourned to April 21st. Thus this great scheme and all its operations are to remain in abeyance for six or seven weeks, when the great question will be in a precisely similar situation to what it is now. We really think that the services of the engineers

might be safely dispensed with, and that they might remain during the summer with the mummies.
(*13 March 1857*)

Stephenson was in Egypt in connection with his great project for a tubular bridge over the Nile. The Bill's passage through Parliament was later held up by Whitsuntide and the Epsom race meeting.

Samuel Smith took a direct part in the proceedings

63

35 The Nene near Horseshoe Corner, looking downstream.
Osborne House is on the extreme right (see plate 42).
20 May 1857 (probably one of the photographs used in the
Parliamentary proceedings).

during the town's opposition to the Bill, when the
Mayor and Town Clerk—

called in as a witness the great luminary of our system,
who will present his testimony before the Committee of
the House of Commons, in such a way as ought to convince
legislators that no futher contribution can be expected
from the port of Wisbech. The assistance of Mr. Samuel
Smith having been invoked for the purpose of obtaining
photographs of the river in its usual state, that gentleman

promptly responded, and has furnished the Parliamentary
Committee with a beautiful set of sun pictures which
convey to the eye most conclusive testimony of the state
of the river. By these calotypes it will be seen that the
shipping trade is at a very low ebb, and that the whole
affair has a very lifeless appearance. The condition of the
town in the neighbourhood of the bridge is also exhibited,
and gives a very fair idea of the present disorganised
state.
(*19 June 1857*)

36 The Nene looking towards Wisbech.
The river looks empty when compared with plate 37, taken from the same spot during the previous year. 20 May 1857 (probably one of the photographs used in the Parliamentary proceedings).

The Bill was thrown out, the preamble not having been proved, and so the photographs were probably not used. It is not definitely known which are the ones that were taken, but it seems likely they included plates 31, 32, 35 and 36.

When the holdup in the works occasioned by the Bill was over, work resumed on the new bridge after a lapse of many months, and—

workmen have this week been employed in weighting the balance end of the bridge with stones. We are informed that it is positively intended to put the bridge over the river on or before the 9th November. If so, the new Mayor, whoever he may be, may have the opportunity of proceeding over it in state, accompanied by his retinue of aldermen and councillors.
(*30 October 1857*)

On Tuesday morning, 3 November, shortly after six—

we were on the spot, where we found the Mayor waiting to witness the important event—for such it really was. After a lapse of a few minutes it was evident that the preparations were complete, and precisely at twenty minutes to seven the bridge was turned across the stream, and safely reached the opposite bank. The Mayor and a portion of the Corporation, accompanied by the Town Chamberlain, were on the bridge at the time it swung round, and were much pleased with the easy and steady motion of the ponderous structure . . . . The bridge remained across the river until four o'clock in the afternoon, when it was brought back into its original position. There is a good deal of work to be done before it will be fit for the whole of the traffic, but it is intended to 'open' the bridge in a more formal manner on Monday next, 9th November.
(*6 November 1857*)

At 11.40 a.m. on 9 November—

the bridge was put over, and the Mayor's carriage dashed across, followed by the carriage of Richard Young, Esq., and by Robert Dawbarn, Esq., on horseback—each of these gentlemen being the first to cross in his own style— the Mayor the first to be driven over, Mr. Young the first to drive over, and Mr. Dawbarn the first to ride over. Immediately afterwards a large body of people from both sides of the river filled the bridge, and for the rest of the day it was thronged, particularly by boys, who seemed to view it as a capital playground constructed for their especial use at a cost of about £15,000. Viewed from the sides of the river, the structure is a most ugly one, but as a public road across the river it certainly is a great improvement upon its predecessor. . . .

The bridge and the machinery for opening it are the work of Messrs. Armstrong & Co. of Elswick Engine Works, Newcastle-on-Tyne, whose hydraulic engines and cranes are now extensively used at the Victoria dock and other places. . . . The building on the south side of the bridge contains the machinery which acts upon the swivel of the bridge. Five or six men are employed to work the hydraulic engine which, by the pressure of water, raises the accumulator—a large perpendicular iron cylinder, loaded to the extent of forty tons; on turning a tap, the pressure of the water is communicated to the cylinder upon which the bridge turns, and the accumulator is then brought to bear upon the chains which turn the whole mass round, so as to make a clear opening up and down the river.
(*13 November 1857*)

Despite progress with the bridge, the other works were beginning to occasion alarm. Dams had been built above the town which were causing the river to silt up, and affecting the supply of fresh water, to the extent that one Wisbech brewer fetched fresh water by lighter from five miles up river. In addition, the improved river course by the bridge had been reduced by a throttle to the same approximate shape as it had been before the work began, and a submerged dam put across. The extra turbulence caused by this device began to affect the warehouses just below the bridge. It is hardly surprising that the people of Wisbech were beginning to tire of the Nene Valley Commissioners and all their works. The bridge, meanwhile, was progressing slowly to completion.

For several weeks the new bridge has been stopped for carriage traffic to allow of the road way and footpaths being laid down with stone and asphalt. . . . The structure is now being painted by Mr. Henry Bell, the colour is as nearly as possible that of a bright iron grey, or of the blue writing paper used for legal and commercial purposes, and has a very good effect.
(*3 September 1858*)

The four new massive stone piers at the corners of the bridge are now completed, and are crowned by handsome lamps. The effect of the piers is to relieve the heaviness of the structure, and greatly to improve the general appearance.
(*3 December 1858*)

The state of the river, caused by the dams and throttle, was so bad that in 1858 the Corporation petitioned the Admiralty, and an enquiry was held. As a result the Commissioners received notice to remove the dams, but refused to do so, and instead applied to Parliament yet again for more money. Eventually the Wisbech Town Council went to court, and on 22 January, 1859, judgement was given in their favour. The people of Wisbech did not wait for the order to be put into effect by the Commissioners, but went immediately to the dams and began to remove them. The Commissioners took legal action, but were unsuccessful, and initiated further proceedings in the Court of Chancery, naming John Gapp, John Gardiner, the newspaper editor, and George Dawbarn, who was soon to become Samuel Smith's brother-in-law. The Bill was dismissed, and great rejoicing greeted the news of the victory in the 'battle of the dams'.

Soon preparations were made for the removal of the throttle at Wisbech, and it was hoped the navigation would now allow ships to get up river through the bridge to the railway, but the bridge was again closed for paving in the middle of 1859, and fears were expressed that the extra weight would prevent it swinging back across the river:

We are informed that great efforts have been made during the past few days to lift the bridge by the hydraulic machinery which the eminent engineers of the Nene Valley Commissioners devised, but hitherto, all efforts have failed.
(*19 August 1859*)

On 29 August the bridge was balanced with thirty-six tons of stones at the weighted end and put back across the river. At the same time the dismantlement of the temporary bridge took place. In May 1860, gas pipes were laid over the iron bridge, preventing it from being opened even if the machinery had been adequate, which it was not:

The engineers said that the bridge could not now be opened; or if opened, that it probably could not be closed again.
(*5 May 1860*)

Some years later, the Admiralty, accepting reality, gave consent for the bridge to become fixed and the ugliness was somewhat lessened by the removal of the counterweight and the tower housing the useless machinery. The iron bridge obstructed shipping more than the old one, as there was less clearance beneath it. It was replaced by a concrete structure in 1931.

The Nene Valley Winding Up Bill, by which the affairs of the Commissioners were finally settled, went through Parliament in the middle of 1862, and the responsibility for the river banks was taken over by the old Commissioners of Sewers. The throttle, which had not been completely removed earlier, was finally dismantled in October 1862 and the materials sold by auction. In the same year a railway branch line opened to the port.

In the latter stages of the works, after the death of Stephenson, the engineer consulted by the Corporation was Thomas Page. In 1860 he produced a report on the improvements in which he suggested, like many others before him, that the river above the bridge should be straightened by a new cut, the Horseshoe bend be by-passed by another new cut, and the old river channel made into a dock. The report was considered by the Town Council in private, but was later published. The proposals were far too expensive to be undertaken, but it seems likely that a series of photographs taken by Smith in September 1861 were intended to illustrate this report. Mounted contemporary prints in the collection of the Kodak Museum are labelled as though they had been exhibited at some time, probably for this purpose, although they could, of course, have been used some years after they were taken to illustrate a later report. Two of the series are illustrated in plates 38 and 39 and show many ships of which the names are known. On 3 October, the *Advertiser* published a list of vessels arriving from foreign parts during September, which included the following:

Name	Tonnage	Cargo	From
Protector	190	Wood	Wyburg
Richard Young	298	,,	,,
Robert James Haynes	206	,,	Gottenburg
Queen	191	,,	Wyburg
Carolina	275	,,	Nyham
Alexandra Mierendorf	216	,,	Soderham
Wardow	199	,,	Onega
John and Eleanor	281	,,	Narva
Ocean	247	,,	Wyburg
Earl Grey	212	,,	Narva

The Robert James Haynes sailed for Calais with a cargo of wheat, but the other ships are not mentioned as having sailed with cargo, and probably all left in ballast.

37 The Nene near Horseshoe Corner, *with the 'Amelia',*
    'Craggs' and 'Vigilant'. The 'Amelia' had arrived from
    Quebec, the others from Wyborg, all with cargoes of timber.
    (cf. plates 21 and 36). 30 August 1856.

38 Wisbech: the Nene. 'No 2 Looking downstream: part of
the river at low water which will form a portion of the
proposed dock.'
*The ships include, left to right, Carolina, Queen,
Alexandra, Robert James Haynes, Protector and
Richard Young.*
*18 September 1861 (This photograph and the next were
probably used to illustrate Thomas Page's report
on the river).*

39 Wisbech: the Nene. 'No 4 Looking upstream: Part of
the river at low water above proposed dock. Vessels at
extreme left hand in distance show the upper end of
bend of river proposed to convert into a dock.'
*The ships include, left to right, John & Eleanor (or
Helena), Earl Grey, Ocean, Meriendorff. No date, but
almost certainly September 1861 (as plate 38).*

40 The Nene near Horseshoe Corner.
*The ship is the 'Hylton' from South Shields. 26 September
1853.*

41 The Nene near Bannister Row, opposite Leverington
    Terrace.
    The 'Lyra' had just arrived from Riga. 2 July 1856.

42 The 'Lady Alice Lambton' screw steamer, *taken the day
before she took about eight hundred people on a day trip to
the mouth of the Humber. She was owned by Richard
Young, whose new home Osborne House can be seen
nearing completion in the background. 8 August 1853.*

Among the many photographs of shipping which do
not appear to have any connection with the river
works is one of the 'Lady Alice Lambton'. The
Advertiser in 1853 announced—

the introduction of a large new iron screw steamer of 700
tons burden to run weekly between Wisbech and the
north, in the coal trade. The spirited individual who is at
the head of the enterprise is Mr. Richard Young, now of

the North Level Sluice, but who will be before long a resident in our suburbs, the field adjacent to the shipyard occupied by Mr. Meadows having been marked out as the site of Mr. Young's future residence.
(*7 January 1853*)

The ship arrived on 28 March, and was greeted by a great crowd after announcement by the Town Crier. She was carrying between five and six hundred tons of coals and was—

by far the largest vessel ever to come up to Wisbech. . . . She was built by Messrs. Marshall of Shields and is sailed by Mr. E. Andrews. Her engine is nominally of 210 horsepower, besides a 'donkey' engine of 8 horsepower for working out her cargo and pumping out the water used for ballast, waterproof bags for that purpose being placed in the bottom of the vessel into which the water is admitted when required. . . . There is no doubt she will be able to carry 700 tons of coals, and there is much discussion as to the probable effect upon the trade of frequent arrivals of such large quantities; some speak of it as the 'ruination' of the port, others are of the opinion that the demand will be commensurate with the supply, and that the trade in coals will extend inland to places which have not been within reach of this port hitherto. . . . The total length of the 'Lady Alice Lambton' is 170 feet, deck 166 feet, breadth 27½ feet, tonnage 600 old measurement, 438 new measurement. With 700 tons of coals on board she will draw 13 feet of water. The first cargo was cleared out by Tuesday night, and the vessel left Wisbech for Sunderland on Wednesday morning. As it takes only six hours to load her, she is expected at Wisbech next Saturday; it is intended to make three voyages, being a total delivery of 2,000 tons of coals, within the fortnight. To commemorate the arrival of the vessel, Mr. Young kindly distributed 1 cwt of the coals to each of the poor inhabitants of Walsoken (in which parish Mr. Young's new residence will be built) to the number of 180.
(*1 April 1853*)

Odd though it may seem to take a day outing on a collier, on 9 August 1853 the same ship—

went out with a 'monster' party, somewhere about 800, we conclude, was the number, but some persons consider there were nearly half as many more, who were conveyed to the mouth of the Humber. The weather was most delightful and all the arrangements were very complete. A great many persons came from Cambridge and other places on the line of railway, by excursion train, and were conveyed back at night. The party were accompanied by Mr. Young, who treated his guests in the most handsome manner.
(*2 September 1853*)

The photograph was taken the day before the outing and shows Young's new home, Osborne House, in the background.

In January 1855 the 'Great Northern' and 'Lady Alice Lambton', both belonging to Young, were chartered for the conveyance of 'navvies' and materials to the Crimea. The latter ship was transferred to Sunderland in November 1856 and in 1862—

came into collision with another vessel a few miles below the Nore, and sunk. The crew were saved.
(*4 October 1862*)

Notice to Passengers.

THE GREAT NORTHERN, Iron Screw Steam Ship, 700 tons burthen, Captain Pinder, and LADY ALICE LAMBTON Iron Screw Steam Ship, 650 tons burthen, Captain Andress, will leave WISBECH for SUNDERLAND, and SUNDERLAND for WISBECH, once or twice every week, and will carry PASSENGERS from one place to the other at the following fares:—

BEST CABIN................ 12s.
FORE CABIN.............. 8s.

For TICKETS apply to Mr. RICHARD YOUNG, WISBECH.

Mr. RICHARD YOUNG

BEGS to inform his friends that, to enable him to meet the Competition of the Railways, he is erecting a LINE OF IRON SCREW STEAM COLLIERS, and the "LADY ALICE LAMBTON" will be ready in three weeks, to run Weekly between SUNDERLAND and WISBECH with best Lambton Wall's-end and Primrose COALS. R. Y. is still open to make Contracts with Merchants and others for Weekly supplies at very reasonable prices.

North Level Sluice, Wisbech, Jan. 31st, 1853.

43 Wisbech: Nene Parade, showing Richard Young's
coalyard.
*The Union Workhouse and Lynn Road eight-sail mill are
in the background. 31 August 1857.*

RETAIL COAL DEPOT.

MR. RICHARD YOUNG,

BEGS to inform the public that he has opened a New Retail Coal Depôt on the Nene Parade, near to Mr.
Boucher's Brewery, where he intends always keeping a Stock of Coals on hand.—Price during the present
week for the best

**LAMBTON PRIMROSE COALS, 16s. 6d. per ton on Carts, or 18s. per ton
delivered to any part of the town.—For Ready Money only.**

ORDERS RECEIVED ON THE PREMISES.

44 The Nene, with the barque 'Richard Young' undergoing repairs on Henson's Slipway. *4 September 1861*.

Richard Young became a considerable shipowner and merchant in Wisbech and took an active part in the affairs of the town. He was Mayor five years in succession between 1858 and 1862, and a member of Parliament for three years from 1865.

His coal yard and some of his other ships can be seen in the photographs. The 'Robert James Haynes', a brig of 206 tons was built at Workington in 1817 and registered at Wisbech in 1845. She had a long and useful life until lost at sea in 1872, all hands being saved. The 'Richard Young', a barque of 298 tons was built at Wisbech in 1849 and sank in the North Sea in 1864.

45 Wisbech: the Nene, *with Henson's Slipway in the background. 25 June 1857.*

46 The Nene below Wisbech, looking towards the town.
*Henson's Slipway can just be seen on the left bank in the
distance. Osborne House is behind the barque in the
foreground. No date (c. 1855).*

47 Wisbech: Bannister Row and the shipyards. *No date
(c. 1855).*

48 Wisbech: a scrapyard near the river bank.
    *The Horseshoe Mill chimney can be seen in the background
    (cf. plate 4). 10 July 1857.*

49 The Nene below Wisbech, looking downstream.
    No date (c. 1854).

50 Wisbech: High Street.
   Parker's hairdressing shop is on the right (detail, figure 16
   and cf. plate 30). A windmill, probably that of J. and
   W. C. Neal, Hill Street, can just be seen behind the Market
   Place. 4 September 1854.

The Town

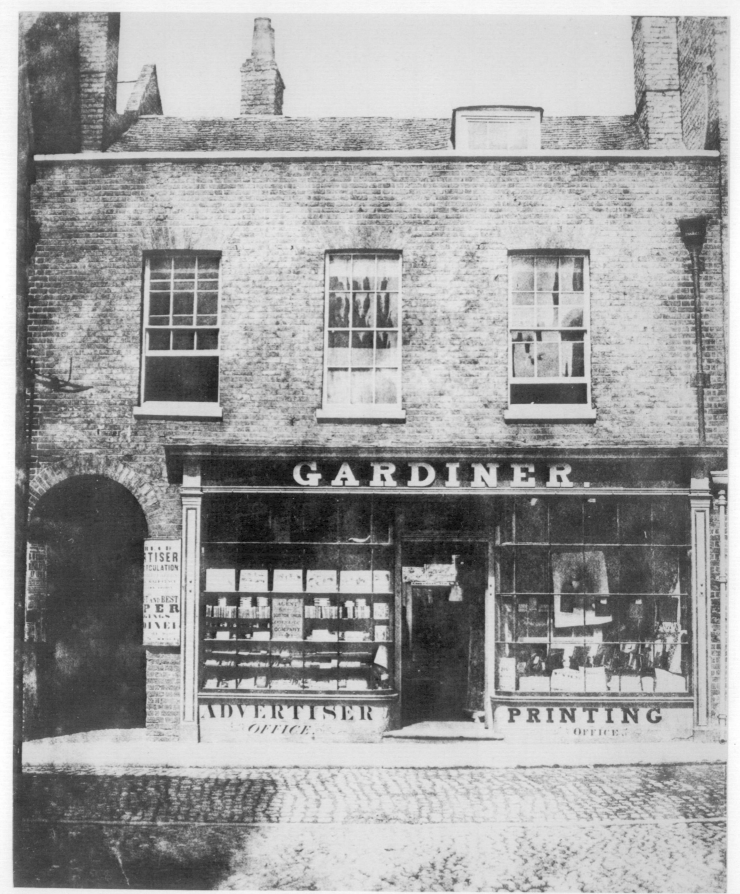

51 Wisbech: Union Street.
John Gardiner's office and shop,
from which the Wisbech Advertiser
was published. 16 June 1858.

THE EXECUTORS OF THE LATE
MR. CHARLES BLAND,
Tea Dealer, Wine & Spirit Merchant,
MARKET PLACE, WISBECH,

BEG to inform the Clergy, Gentry, and the Public generally, that they have disposed of the above Business to Mr. NELSON FOSTER, whose experience in the different branches of the Business, and strict attention to its duties, will enable him with care and punctuality to execute any commands with which he may be favored.

NELSON FOSTER,

In succeeding to the Business of the late Mr. Charles Bland, respectfully solicits from the Clergy, Gentry, and Inhabitants generally in the surrounding Neighbourhood, a continuance of the patronage bestowed upon his Predecessor, and trusts by punctuality and personal attention, to retain the connection unimpaired.

Wisbech, April 27th, 1854.

J. G. BARLEY,
(Late *GROUNDS,*)
Family and Dispensing Chemist,
Wholesale and Retail Druggist, Oil and Colorman, and Dealer in Patent Medicines,
(Two doors from the Rose and Crown Hotel,)
Market Place, Wisbech,

IN returning his very sincere thanks to his numerous friends for the liberal support conferred upon him during the sixteen years he resided in the Old Market, respectfully informs them and the public generally of Wisbech and its neighbourhood, that his Business is now ENTIRELY REMOVED to the Shop in the Market Place, so many years conducted by the late Mr. GROUNDS, and latterly by Mr. HOLLINGWORTH, where he intends to endeavour to deserve their continued patronage, by strict personal attention, a careful selection of every article requisite in his business, and punctuality in executing all orders committed to his care.

Prescriptions will receive the promptest attention.

Genuine Colza Oil for Moderator Lamps, and other Lamp Oils of the best quality only—at moderate prices.

Pickling Vinegar, Sauces, Cigars, &c.

Barley's Noted Horse Medicines, Cattle Drinks, and Sheep Ointment.

Godfrey's Balls always ready.

⁂ Agent for Crews's Disinfecting Fluid. Patterson's Smut Eradicator. Down's Farmer's Friend. White and Fairchild's Turkey Coffee, &c.

☞ Excepting in cases of necessity, No Business done on Sundays.

Market Place, October, 1854.

51 Wisbech: Union Street.
John Gardiner's office and shop,
from which the Wisbech Advertiser
was published. 16 June 1858.

84

52 Wisbech: Market Place.
Barley and Foster moved here from the Old Market and Cornhill after their old premises had been demolished (cf. plates 23 and 24). 6.30 am, 15 June 1857.

Many of Smith's photographs of buildings in Wisbech show the same concern with change which is such an important part of his work. Even a photograph like that of the Market Place, which seems merely a general view with no other motive, shows the shops of Barley and Foster who moved there from Cornhill when their premises were demolished.

53 Wisbech: Parish church of St Peter and St Paul. *6 June 1853.*

A more direct and obvious record of change is present in the photographs of Wisbech parish church, which include 'before and after' views of the extensive restoration which took place during the 1850's.

In September 1853 an appeal was launched for funds to restore St Peter's Church and, after considerable delays, tenders were invited in July 1855 and the work carried out between March 1856 and January 1857.

The architects were George Glover of Lowestoft and William Smith of Adelphi, London. Most of the restoration was to the interior, but the east end exterior and the churchyard were also considerably altered.

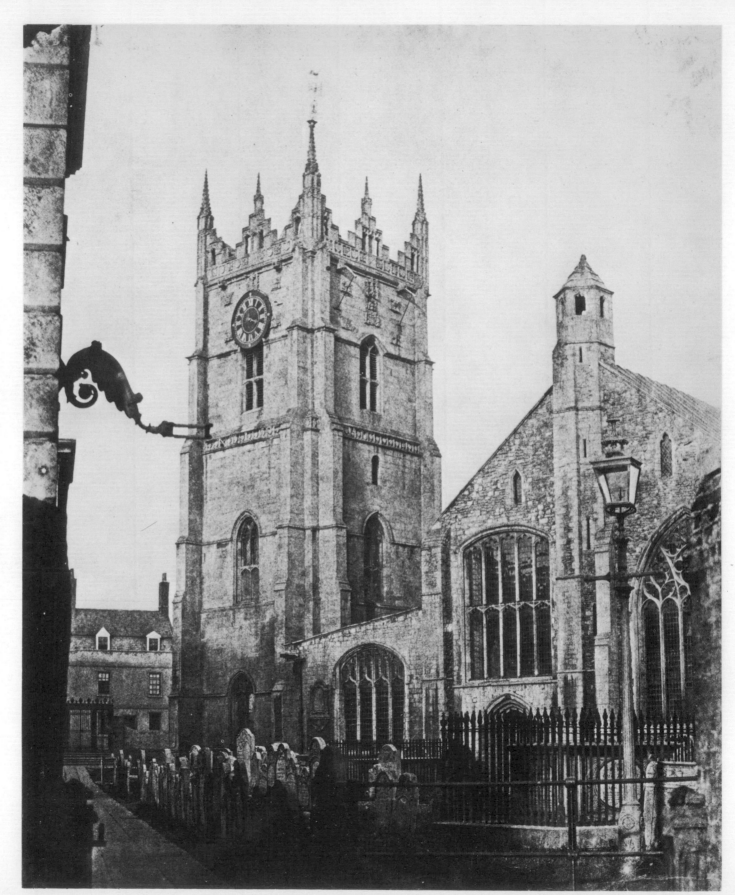

54 Wisbech: the parish church.
*The west end, showing the early
sixteenth-century window,
replaced in 1861. No date (c. 1855).*

55 Wisbech: the parish church, *showing the east end before restoration. No date (c. 1854).*

The new window of the church was designed by W. Smith, Esq., of London, architect, and executed by Mr. Ringham of Ipswich, the contractor for the restoration and improvement of the church. The stained glass is by Messrs. Hardman of Birmingham, and fully maintains the reputation of these gentlemen. . . . It has been erected by G. Cottam, Esq., to the memory of his son. The cost of this magnificent gift, so appropriate an ornament to the church, is nearly £400.
(*14 November 1856*)

The far more attractive original window can be seen on the 'before' photograph. The restoration did, however, open up a good Perpendicular window in the south Chancel which had been bricked up. It is almost certain that the drawing of the church which appeared in the *Advertiser* of 7 March was taken from Smith's photograph.

The west end of the church also underwent less

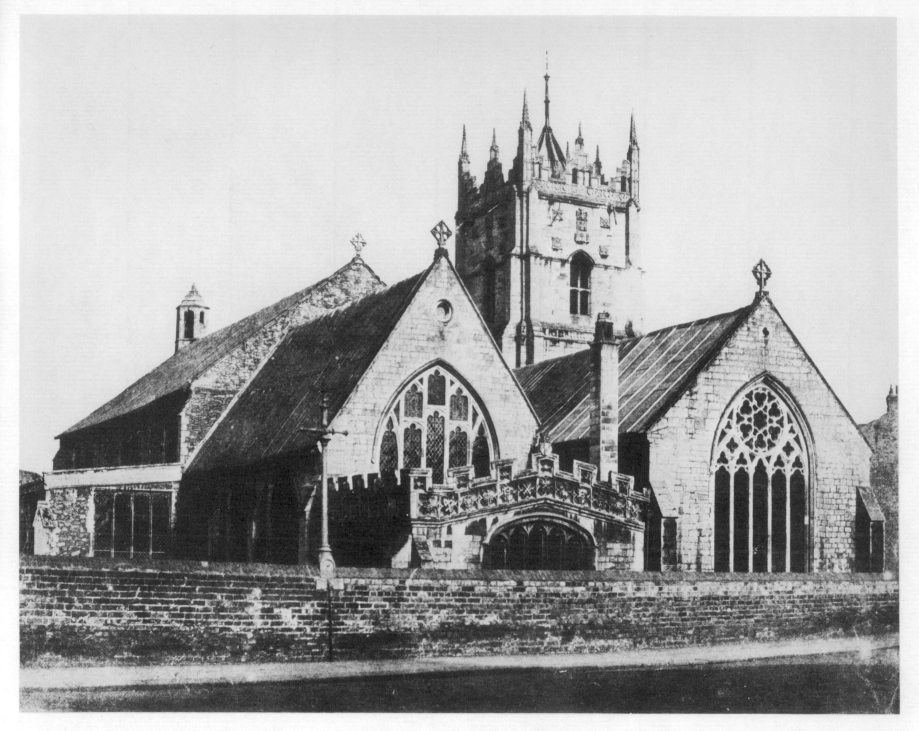

56 Wisbech: the parish church, *showing the east end after restoration. One chancel east window has been renewed and the other unblocked. A 'before and after' pair with plate 55. 6.15 am, 15 June 1857.*

extensive alterations a few years later, in 1861:

> A handsome memorial window has just been placed in our Parish Church. It occupies a place over the west door, and is substituted for a very large plain perpendicular window which was out of place and a great eyesore. The design of the stonework is early English, and is furnished by W. Smith, Esq., architect. It is admirably suited to the church and to the place where it appears.
> (*24 October 1861*)

No photograph by Samuel Smith of the new window is known. It is in fact a rather mean interpretation of the Decorated style which bears no comparison with the magnificent genuine specimen next to it, or even the early sixteenth-century window it replaced.

57 Wisbech: North Brink.
The Exchange Hall, before alteration, is in the right foreground. The low building with dormer windows on the far left is the old Friends' Meeting House. 6 June 1853.

The North Brink was photographed many times by Smith and, apart from the river works, two main changes appear on them. The less obvious is the rebuilding of the Friends' Meeting House to designs by Algernon Peckover, Smith's friend and a millionaire member of an important local banking family.

It appears to have been originally two cottages, converted to its present use in 1711.
(W&C p. 389)

The Friends' Meeting House on the North Brink, a very humble looking structure, has just been pulled down, and the first stone of a new one has been laid upon the same site.
(*May 1854*)

It has been lately rebuilt in a simple style of architecture; and it is not generally known that in a small garden attached to it repose the remains of one of the descendants of the royal and unfortunate Stuarts.
(*7 May 1856*)

58 Wisbech: North Brink.
The Exchange Hall has been altered by opening up the three central arches for access to the new Corn Exchange behind. The Friends' Meeting House has been rebuilt (cf. plates 12 and 13). The temporary wooden bridge is still in existence. 25 July 1859.

More evident from the photographs is the change in the front of the Exchange Hall, which—

was built in 1811. . . . The site was then occupied by a public house called the Nag's Head. It was built somewhat after the manner of the Custom House [that is, the Butter Cross], being two second storey rooms raised upon five open arches in front. . . . The lower storey was at first filled up with stalls as a corn exchange, which stalls were let at £3 3s. per year, but the buyers and sellers soon

mutually deserted the public system of doing business, and preferred a more free and easy system of bargaining than the restrictions of stallage offered. It therefore happened that very soon after the Corn Exchange was erected, its purpose was superseded, as the farmers and merchants preferred the open hill in front of the exchange. . .

It retained its character, though deserted as an Exchange, till 1831, when the lower apartment, or proper Exchange, was let for one pound per year for five years, the hirer agreeing to fit it up at his own expense as a room for public

59 Wisbech: North Brink above the Meeting House, *which can just be seen on the extreme right. Both it and the houses next door with the stepped 'Jacobean' gables were designed by Algernon Peckover. 9 May 1859.*

and other meetings, assemblies, the performance of concerts, delivery of lectures, public exhibitions, respectable auctions, public library or bazaar, to the satisfaction of the Capital Burgesses. Since this date it has been used exclusively for the above purposes and has been a great accommodation to the town.
(W&C pp. 427–8)

A few years later, the wheel had turned full circle, and a limited company was formed in 1857 for the purpose

of establishing a Corn Exchange. It was agreed that the Company should rent the lower floor of the Exchange Hall and erect a building behind the Exchange at a cost of not less than £1,500.

Progress was swifter than usual in Wisbech, and early the following year the Exchange was rapidly advancing.

Access will be gained to the building by the doors in the

60 Wisbech: North Brink.
The Exchange Hall and
National Provincial Bank.
25 July 1859.

61 Wisbech: the Chapel of Ease, or Octagon Church, Old Market. *No date* (*c. 1853*).

vestibule which comprises the middle portion of the old Exchange Hall.
(*5 February 1858*)

The new Exchange was opened on 29 July 1858. Many of the Wisbech photographs could be used to illustrate Craddock and Walker's *History*, and it is quite possible that Smith used the book as a source of subject matter. It is full of lively criticism of the

buildings of the neighbourhood, both old and new, including the Church, Bridge and Butter Cross, which have already been dealt with, and the Chapel of Ease, Workhouses and Cemetery Chapel which follow.

The Chapel of Ease, or Octagon Church, which stood in the Old Market was built in 1826. The cost—

estimated at £7,500, was proposed to be defrayed by shares of £50 each to be repaid by the letting of sittings:

62 Wisbech: Lynn Road with the eight-sail mill.
No date (c. 1853).

£6,000 was quickly raised by this means, and the building was entrusted to Mr. William Swansborough as architect. It happened, unfortunately, that the period of erecting this chapel was a period in which the true principles of Gothic architecture were ill understood. . . . The form adopted is that of an octagon, with an elongation of its eastern side for a chancel, and of the lower storey of its west front for a porch. . . . The architect placed an octagonal lantern upon the roof and rising to the height of 26 feet above it, but the difficulty of providing adequate support for such a feature in such a situation made it fall into comparatively early decay; and in 1846, the chapel wardens came to the resolution of removing it, and substituting the present low embattled termination, designed by Mr. Buckler. . . . The Chapel is built of brick, faced in some parts with stone and plaster. It cost altogether about £10,000. . . . The octagon at Ely is the praise of the world; the octagon at Wisbech is fortunately unknown, except to its inhabitants.
(W&C *pp. 383–5*)

63 Wisbech: Albion Place, the Old Workhouse.
Built in 1720–2, it was replaced soon after 1835 and subdivided into smaller premises, including the Custom House which had at one time occupied the Butter Cross. 4 September 1854.

The Old Workhouse on Albion Place was built in 1720-2.

'*Nov 14 1720. It was agreed that the Town Bailiff do cause 260,000 of bricks to be made for the use of the town, in order to build a workhouse. Ye bricks to be made on three acres of town land.*'

A year elapsed in this work, when the Corporation resolved '*that a workhouse about 110 feet square, in a place called ye Hors Fare, be Built, and yt in order thereto, the Town Bailiff may procure upon ye Town seal a sum of money not exceeding one thousand pounds.*'

This sum was increased eleven months afterwards (Oct 1722) by another thousand pounds borrowed in the same manner. This continued to be the house that 'held the parish poor' till the passing of the recent Poor Law Act, when it was sold for £1,700 some time after the erection of the Union Workhouse on Lynn Road. (W&C pp. 424–5, quoting the Town Records)

64 Wisbech: the Union Workhouse, Lynn Road.
20 September 1853.

The Union Workhouse—

which was erected after the passing of the new Poor Law Act in 1835, is the Poor-house for 22 parishes. It is built in an ornamental manner on Lynn Road, . . . is calculated to accommodate 600 persons, and consists internally of a board-room, two school rooms, waiting hall, dining hall, register room, receiving wards, shoemaker's and tailor's shops, two sick wards, two hospitals, ten sitting rooms, twenty three bedrooms, four clothing stores, two oakum

sheds, kitchens, &c. The style adopted is that called Elizabethan, though Stuart architecture would perhaps more appropriately denominate its degenerate degeneracy. . . . There is a neat lodge in the same style next the road, and a wide, clean, gravelled path, and evergreens which fill the considerable space in front, give the whole rather the appearance of an opulent private mansion than a parish poor-house.
(W&C *pp. 430–1*)

65 Wisbech: the General Cemetery, Leverington Road, *where Samuel Smith's first wife was buried a few months before this photograph was taken, and Smith himself was finally laid to rest in 1892. The Chapel was built in 1848 to the designs of William Adams. 23 July 1856.*

The General Cemetery was established in 1836.

The principle of its establishment is the most liberal, Churchman or Dissenter of any sect may be interred according to his own peculiar ceremonies without any restraint or interference. . . . The Committee in 1848 came to the resolution of erecting a chapel for reading the funeral service, and for other public business connected with the Cemetery. . . . A very neat chapel, from a design by Mr. Adams, has accordingly been erected, being partly brickwork, partly plaster, partly stone. The style is classic. . . . It forms a very pleasing as well as necessary addition to the beauties of the ground.
(W&C *pp. 494–5*)

This photograph is one of a series taken by Smith. Some of them show his first wife's grave, in which he himself was later buried.

The tall column in the background is not, as one might expect, a monument to some eminent Wisbech

66 Wisbech: the old Gasworks, Leverington Road.
*The foundation stone was laid in 1832. The building is
similar in style to the nearby Cemetery Chapel. No date.*

Victorian, but the chimney of the old Gas Works on
Leverington Road.

Because of great dissatisfaction with the supply of
gas, which was privately supplied from the old Works
by Mr Malam, the proprietor, a group of local men
decided to set up a rival Wisbech Gas Light and Coke
Company. In September 1859 the new company
completely took over supply of gas, and the *Advertiser*
reported an almost immediate improvement in

quality. By this time, a new works had been constructed across the river in Eastfield, and at the 1862
annual meeting of the Company—

Mr. Pattrick asked what the directors intended to do with
the old Gas Works. The Chairman intimated that the
property had been offered for sale without success, that in
the present state of the town he thought it inadvisable to
force a sale, but that better times might be looked for
when something like the value might be realised.
(*11 September 1862*)

67 Wisbech: Leverington Road Toll Bar, with Mr Marshall George Strapps, Toll keeper. *9 May 1859.*

The Leverington Road toll bar lay between Malvern House and Wisbech, and Smith probably passed it frequently. The toll-collector, Marshall George Strapps, was something of a local celebrity: he—

employed his leisure time in acquiring the art of wood carving, and although entirely self-taught, he has produced work which is highly creditable . . . five medals having been awarded to him at exhibitions in London, Norwich, Wisbech and elsewhere for meritorious work.

Mr. Strapps, who was formerly a postman, and custodian of the Wisbech Institute, has now retired from active life, but is a collector of coins and curios of various kinds. (G *pp. 83–4*)

It is easy to imagine Samuel Smith stopping for a few words with Mr Strapps on the way into Wisbech. A number of his carvings can still be seen at the Institute and there is a fine model windmill in the Museum.

68 Wisbech: Webster's Mill, Leverington Road.
A mill was in existence on the site in 1712 and came into the hands of the Webster family at the end of the eighteenth century. The post mill was demolished late in the nineteenth century. No date (c. 1856).

The turnpike roads were gradually taken over by the local authorities until by about 1880 they had completely disappeared; but at the time the photograph was taken, the people of Wisbech were—

now hedged in by toll-bars on every side, no other town in the kingdom probably being burdened in the same proportion and deriving so little benefit.
(*27 February 1857*)

Elsewhere

Smith also travelled with his camera, and an extensive series of photographs of the churches and cathedrals of the Fenland exists, as well as a few showing other features. The most interesting of the latter are of Hunstanton Hall, Norfolk, just after the disastrous fire of 1853 which destroyed nearly twenty rooms, including the ancient dining room, the ballroom and the state bedroom (Plate 83).

The series of churches is more typical of amateur nineteenth-century photography, and not perhaps of so much interest as his other work. The series does, however, include his finest photograph: that of Ely Cathedral (Plate 76), a masterpiece of the art which will withstand any comparison.

The passages which accompany the following plates have been taken, wherever possible, from sources more or less contemporary with the photographs.

It is impossible to know what Samuel Smith's intentions were when he took up photography. Unfortunately, no diary has survived, although he was the type of person who may well have kept at least a technical notebook.

It is likely he started out to take views such as those of his own village and the Fenland churches, which would have appealed to his personal and antiquarian tastes. When the river works began, not only did he have a good vantage point from the bank a few yards from his front door, but also the means to record the changes which were occurring there and in nearby Wisbech. We have every reason to be grateful that Samuel Smith, probably encouraged by Thomas Craddock, realized the potential of his photographic hobby in that situation and used it to such good effect.

69 West Walton: St Mary's Church. *2 June 1857.*

The Church—

is its most attractive antiquity. Though now in a state of wretched desolation—the effect of long misuse and the want of proper renovation at the proper time—it renders in every part a perfect notion of what it was in its days of perfection. The tower, which first meets the eye of the stranger as he turns the road that leads to the Church, attracts his notice, not less for its beautiful workmanship than for its standing insulated [sic] from the Church. . . . It

is a very fine specimen of Early English workmanship. . . . The principal external object on the south side of the church is an Early English porch of fine but delapidated workmanship and design.
(W&C *pp. 513–4*)

West Walton

70 West Walton: St Mary's Church, south porch.
    18 April 1854.

71 Tydd St Giles Church.
   Together the two photographs form a panoramic view.
   Samuel Smith was born in Tydd St Giles.
   19 September 1853.

Tydd St Giles

The Church—

is a neat structure, with a square embattled tower, . . . [standing] about fifty feet from the body of the Church at the east end, which is very unusual. The pillars of the nave incline to the west, which induces some persons to suppose that a tower did once support that end of the church. . . . The chancel is a modern erection, built about seventy years since, when particular attention was given to discover whether the present tower was ever

connected with the Church, but the foundation showed no marks that any former building ever existed to unite the tower therewith.
(W&C p. 534)

The photographs are interesting in that they form a panorama of two views taken from the same spot (see figure 11, page 20).

The eighteenth-century chancel, demolished soon after this photograph was taken, was so small that it cannot be seen from this viewpoint.

72 Tydd St Mary's Church,
Lincolnshire. *31 May, 1859.*

Tydd St Mary

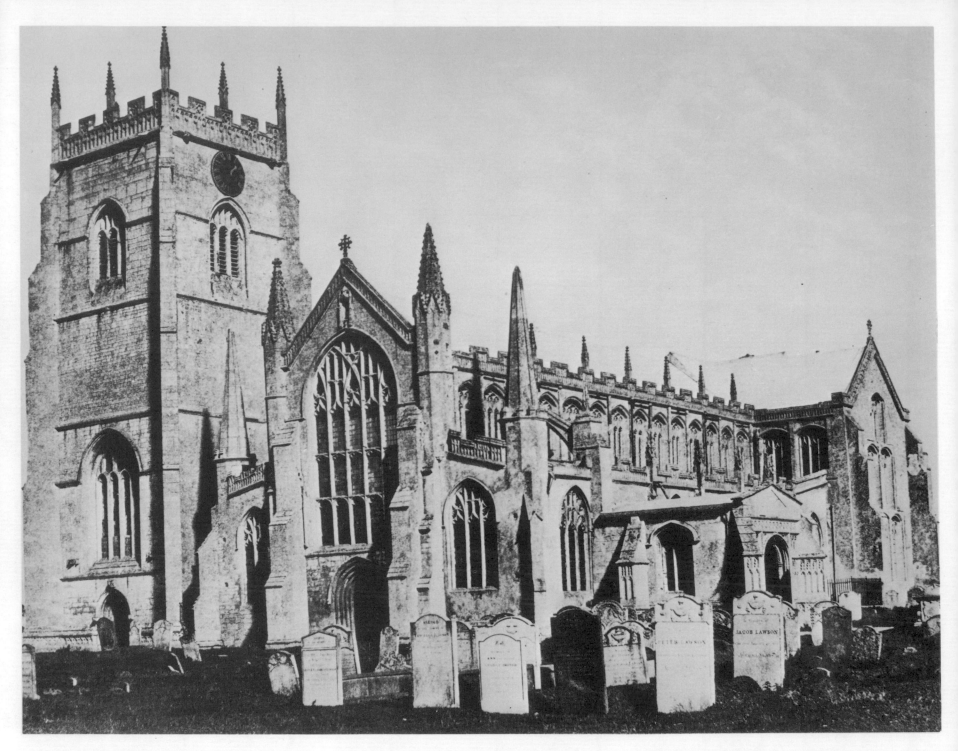

Tydd St Mary lies adjacent to Tydd St Giles, but across the border into Lincolnshire.

The church of St Mary is an old building in the Gothic style, with a square tower (containing five bells) and a beautiful spire; a handsome window has been placed in the chancel by the rector.
(*1853 Post Office Directory*)

The new window, which replaced one that had been blocked up, is seen resplendent at the east end.

Terrington St Clement is a village, parish and station on the Lynn and Sutton Bridge Railway, 5 miles west from Lynn by ferry and 6½ by road, and 10 miles north-east from Wisbech. . . .
The Church of St Clement is a spacious cruciform structure of freestone, in the Perpendicular style, consisting of chancel, nave, aisle and transept, with a massive detached tower at the north-west angle containing six bells; it was erected in 1380, and repaired, new roofed, and the lofty pinnacles restored in 1829. . . .
(*Kelly's Post Office Directory, 1879*)

73 Terrington St Clement's Church, Norfolk.
In this photograph, which is a copy from an original print, a separate cloud negative has been used. No date.

Terrington St Clement

74 Newton, Isle of Ely: the Rectory. *24 September 1862.*

Newton is a Parish and picturesque village in the Isle of Ely, situated on the Norfolk border of the county, 4 miles north from Wisbech Great Eastern Station. . . . The living is a rectory . . . held by Rev. George Elwes Corrie, D.D., Master of Jesus College, Cambridge.
(*Kelly's Post Office Directory, 1879*)

In the photograph is one of Smith's rare figures, posed beside the handsome late Georgian building. Dr Corrie was rector in 1862, but probably did not live in the village. The lady is therefore likely to be the wife of one of the curates.

Newton

Peterborough is an ancient city . . . situated on the northern bank of the river Nene, which divides it from Huntingdonshire, and is at the south-eastern extremity of the county of Northampton. . . .

The Cathedral Church of St. Peter, supposed to have been commenced about the year 1118, is a noble structure, partly in the Norman and partly in the Early English style, giving evidence of at least eight periods of construction . . . The most conspicuous feature of this building is the west front:

the plan consists of three arches 82 feet in height, the middle one being considerably narrower than the others. . . . At either extremity are two lofty turrets . . . [which] connect the arcade with the wall of the church. . . .

The Market House, in the Market Place, is an ancient building, and bears date 1671: it is now used as the butter and poultry market.
(Post Office Directory 1869)

75 **Peterborough: the Market Place.** *The seventeenth-century Guildhall is on the left, raised on open arches. It faces the gateway of the Cathedral behind which rises the magnificent west front, built about 1200. No date (c. 1860).*

Peterborough

111

76 Ely Cathedral.
Smith's photographs of Ely are among the very few in existence which show the octagon lantern before the extensive restoration by Scott. 20 April 1854.

Ely, a city, bishop's see . . . and capital of the Isle of its name, is seated in the middle of the shire of Cambridge. . . . The Cathedral here is an object of great admiration from its antiquity and beauty: there is no cathedral in England possessing finer examples of the successive styles of architecture. . . .
(*Kelly's Post Office Directory 1879*)

The series of views of Ely, taken early in Smith's career, contain some of his best work. The photographs are valuable also in that they show the Octagon as restored by Essex in about 1756, before Sir George Gilbert Scott's thorough restoration of about 1860. It is on the Ely Octagon that the Wisbech Octagon Church was originally based (plate 61).

A camera, possibly Craddock's, can be seen in plate

Ely

77 Ely Cathedral. *20 April 1854.*

78 **Ely Cathedral,** *with a calotype camera in the foreground.*
20 April 1854.

78; perhaps it took the photograph which was the
subject of the following news item, but which cannot
now be traced:

Mr Craddock, of this town, has been requested by Prince
Albert to forward to Windsor Castle a copy of the photo-
graphic view of Ely Cathedral, as exhibited by
Mr Craddock at the Photographic Exhibition, Pall Mall,
London.
(*Wisbech Advertiser, 22 March 1855*)

Croyland Abbey, the ruins of which stand on an island in the Lincolnshire Fens, was founded in 716 to commemorate the place where St Guthlac made his habitation. After the Dissolution—

the choir and transepts were taken down; and the nave and aisles suffered to remain as a place of devotion for the use of the parish. . . . In the Parliamentary War, the army under Cromwell pressed the town so closely that the people

79 Crowland, Lincolnshire: Croyland Abbey from the south east.
In the foreground is a small sapling, not another calotype camera. 23 June 1859.

Crowland

sought refuge in the tower of the church, which in those times was considered a parochial fortress, and in the attack that was made upon the sacred edifice, the nave and south aisle were so much injured that they soon fell into a state of delapidation.

... [At the north west] is a tower and spire of clumsy and inelegant proportions of late Perpendicular date. ... The other part of the west front, which formed the west end of the nave is a magnificent specimen of architectural embellishment, of different periods of Gothic. The entrance first attracts the attention of the visitors; this consists of a deeply moulded single arch, enclosing two smaller ones with a quatrefoil in the spandrel; in the latter are sculpted remarkable events which occurred to St Guthlac. ... Above this door has been a noble window, now alas! without mullions or tracery! But here are four tiers of statues occupying niches which remain in tolerable preservation, ...

The whole of the nave and south aisle is one mess of ruins; they contain however some good remains of Norman and Early English architecture. The north aisle remains very nearly in its original state.

('*Lincolnshire Churches, Division of Holland*', *1843, printed and published by T. N. Morton, Boston*)

Crowland is also celebrated for its triangular bridge. Formerly the Welland divided into two streams, one branch leading to the Nene, and the other continuing to Spalding. A stream of water was diverted from the river through the Abbey grounds past the slaughter house and offices. Three roads crossed over these streams, one for Peterborough, one for Peakirk and Stamford, and one for Spalding and the Abbey. These three roads, each by a separate arch, met at the centre of the bridge. The channel of the Nene branch of the Welland has long been filled in, and the stream which passed to the Abbey ground is enclosed by a culvert. The bridge is 8 ft. wide and therefore only adapted for horse or foot passengers.

('*A History of the Fens of South Lincolnshire*' *by W. H. Wheeler, 2nd Ed. (1897), p. 313. The book was originally published in 1868*)

80 Crowland: Croyland Abbey. *The west door, with a figure, probably Thomas Craddock, leaning on the gate. No date.*

81 Crowland:
Croyland Abbey, west front.
*The calotype camera in the foreground
almost certainly belonged to
Thomas Craddock. 19 April 1855.*

82 Crowland: the Triangular Bridge. *23 June 1859.*

83 Hunstanton Hall, Norfolk,
after the fire of 1853.
11 July 1853.

Hunstanton

84 Hunstanton: the Lighthouse. *19 July 1853.*

Hunstanton is a parish, village and healthful sea-bathing place . . . 17 miles north-by-east from Lynn . . . in the western division of the county [of Norfolk], . . . The sands extend 3 miles, and sea-bathing is safe and agreeable . . .

Near the highest point of the cliff is the lighthouse, a substantial building, which was completed in 1840, rising upward of 50 feet, erected by the Trinity House, the light exhibited is on the catoptrical principle, and can be seen on dark nights, with a clear atmosphere, at a distance of 18 or 20 miles, from the decks of vessels, . . .

The Hall is situated in a beautifully wooded park, and is the seat of Hamon L'Estrange, Esq.; this fine mansion, in 1853, was much injured by fire; the ancient baronial banquet hall and 18 other rooms were destroyed.

(Kelly's Post Office Directory, 1879)

PLAN
OF THE TOWN OF
WISBECH
WITH
NEW WALSOKEN
FROM
ACTUAL SURVEY
BY
FRED. J. UTTING.
OCTOBER 1848